PSYCHO DOG

For Hugh, with love from all the dogs!

PSYCHO DOG

All your dog problems answered
in one easy-to-follow guide

Janet Menzies

Quiller

First published in the UK in 2016 by
Quiller, an imprint of Quiller Publishing Ltd

British Library Cataloguing-in-Publication Data
A catalogue record for this book is available from
the British Library

ISBN 978-1-84689-237-0

Printed in Malaysia
Edited by Paul Middleton
Jacket designed by Arabella Ainslie
Book designed by Guy Callaby

Quiller

An imprint of Quiller Publishing Ltd
Wykey House, Wykey, Shrewsbury SY4 1JA
Tel: 01939 261616 Fax: 01939 261606
E-mail: info@quillerbooks.com
Website: www.quillerpublishing.com

The Problem Solver:
Where to find your problem

THE ENDEARING PROBLEMS

THE IRRITATING PROBLEMS

THE SOCIAL PROBLEMS

THE HEALTH-RELATED PROBLEMS

THE SERIOUS PROBLEMS

Contents

Acknowledgements

My thanks go to Andrew and Gilly Johnston and everybody at Quiller Publishing who picked up the idea for this book and ran with it so enthusiastically. The illustrations are a very important part of the book, and Nige Burr of www.nigeburrphotography.co.uk did brilliantly in capturing much of the psycho behaviour described. He also managed to do the author cover photograph without breaking too many lenses. Thank you to *Condé Nast* for permission to reproduce Danny Shanahan's 'Lassie: Get Help', from the *New Yorker* magazine. Others who have contributed photographs are Sharon Hardy of www.hibirdphotography. co.uk; Anabelle Other; Marco Soppelsa; Jennifer Hirsch of

www.beautybotanist.com; Will Forbes, farrier; Joe Welling, farrier; Caroline Blackwood; Sherina Balaratnam of www.sthetics.co.uk; and Anita Jones. Thanks also to Duncan Fraser, who helps with my dogs when I go down with one of my many sporting injuries. I think my main qualification for writing *Psycho Dog* is that I have made pretty much every mistake described in the book at least once. So my enduring gratitude goes to all the many top professional dog trainers who have helped me over the years, and are essentially the authors of the solutions in this book. The dog community is wonderfully welcoming and supportive, and more than makes up for any psycho-issues you may be experiencing with your dog.

jigeburrphotography.co.uk

Introduction

When it comes to analysing your psycho dog, there is a wonderful cartoon that so nearly says it all, so I almost didn't have to write this book. As you can see, the first scene shows the typical *Lassie* scenario: needless to say, a human is drowning in a lake, while his faithful border collie, Lassie, looks on from the bank. Thrashing about madly, the human yells to his dog: 'Lassie! Get help!' So off Lassie dutifully goes, and there we see him in the next picture, lying at full stretch on the psychiatrist's couch, gesticulating with his paw as he explains all to the analyst. As instructed, loyal Lassie is getting help. It is perhaps unfortunate for his owner that intelligent Lassie has understood that the help he needs is that of a professional psycho-dog-analyst.

Danny Shanahan captures Lassie's much-needed visit to the psycho-dog-analyst.

I'm sure the human manages to get himself out of the water – he's only yards from the edge after all! And I can just imagine what Lassie is saying as he lays on the psychiatrist's couch: 'Well, you see, I'm having terrible trouble with my humans. They keep getting themselves into all sorts of mad scrapes and I have to rescue them every time. It's like they can't take any responsibility at all for their own lives. It's just one thing after another – mineshafts, rip tides, burglars, evil property developers, runaway horses, train tracks ... I mean, honestly, Doc, it's really doing my head in. The responsibility of it all is just too much for me. You know, by the time I get home, I will be expected to sort the next thing out, and at the end of the day, I'm just a dog, I've only got paws.'

So, as you rush to condemn your dog and his behaviour as psycho, it's a good idea to take a moment to see the other side of the story. It will also help give you a wider perspective on the whole situation. Yes, you may have a problem with your dog. Don't worry. It's not the end of the world. It's not global warming. It's not dieting. It's not even terrorism – though it may feel like it sometimes. There is hope! Everything will be OK in the end.

Please bear this in mind when your dog steals and eats every crumb of the lemon tart that was going to be the highlight of your dinner party. Lyn (FTCh Kelmscott Whizz) did that to me. Or if the dog knows exactly when next door is going to put out the rubbish bags and makes that the precise moment it escapes the house-sitter (thank you, Dutch) – try not to get too bothered. Or if the Labrador pulls so hard your daughter trips over the kerb and loses a tooth (not one of my dogs on this occasion), just head for the dentist and then buy this book on the way back. It is all solvable and there will be a time when you look back on all this and laugh about it, even if through a gritted new front tooth.

For an author, having a problem dog is actually better than having a perfect dog, because it gives you a lot more to write about – even if it's only amusing anecdotes for your readers. For example, writing about my saintly spaniel, Ricky, is fairly predictable: 'Got up; Ricky wagged tail and grinned; walked dogs; Ricky kept coming back with presents for me; fed dogs; Ricky sat quietly and waited patiently for his turn.' Yawn. Whereas there is a lot more to say about Solo: 'Got up; Solo burst out of his dog bed and nicked Lemon's toy before she could stop him, then did three laps of the lawn waving it at her; walked dogs; Solo shot off in hot pursuit of a rabbit; told him off and called him back; Solo grinned and wagged tail, he's obviously planning to do it all again tomorrow.' But there is a truth hidden in this, that challenging dogs are often very rewarding dogs. If you've been through some difficult times together, you eventually reach an understanding that has an immense amount of shared experience in it. You become comrades, even if the ride has been rocky.

Problems can be amusing as well as annoying – but that doesn't mean we shouldn't bother to solve them. My friend's daughter's front tooth was expensive to replace, and the incident was totally preventable if the dog had been taught not to pull on the lead in the first place. This book will show you how to get the best out of the dog, at the same time as allowing his wonderful character to shine through. You will find you end up with the best of all friends – a dog with

(Left) Ricky demonstrating what a good dog he is.

(Right) Ricky bringing me a present.

nigeburrphotography.co.uk

the intelligence to have his own identity, and the loving obedience to share it with you in a positive way.

The most common issues I come across with dogs or that my readers report to me are minor and easy to cure. Pulling on the lead is the number one dog problem people ask me about. In the greater perspective of all the ghastly things that go wrong in life, often on a daily basis, the dog pulling on the lead is really not up there. Better yet, it is very easy to solve, as this book will show you. Most of what you will be discovering is a simple, basic understanding of how a dog's mind works, how a human's mind works – and importantly, how to get them both working in the same direction!

Fortunately for us as dog owners, there is only one dog problem that is really, truly serious, and that is a dog that attacks humans or animals. For safety's sake, there is a short 'emergency guide' in the next section of this book just in case, in addition to the discussion and solutions outlined in *Part Two*.

Over the last couple of decades, animal behaviourists have been able to put a great deal of science behind our understanding of dog behaviour. It is fascinating, for

Solo heading out to do naughtiness all over again tomorrow.

example, to realise that rewarding good behaviour works because it is actually physically creating new neural pathways in the dog's brain that will gradually overtake the previous 'bad' connections. This allows the old pathways to die back or atrophy, so establishing the new good behaviour permanently. We now know a lot more about how this works scientifically, but the teaching techniques we use are still instantly recognisable as common sense, effectiveness-based methods. So this book will concentrate on giving you the quick, simple solution to your dog problem that you want. Then, once the initial chaos of the dog chasing next door's pet rabbit has been dealt with, I hope you will enjoy reading the science bit at the back of the book.

First of all, congratulate yourself on having taken the very positive and important steps of both recognising there is a problem, and even more sensibly, deciding to do something about it. Just those two actions in themselves more or less guarantee success. The unvarnished truth about most dog problems is that they continue purely and simply because the humans involved don't bother to do anything about them. Either we go into denial – the 'he's only playing' syndrome. Or we know there is a problem with the dog and just don't really care enough. Dog owners constantly complain to me that their dogs chew, bark, run off, bother visitors, steal food or growl, and basically just rule the house. Yet they don't actually do anything about it.

I find this puzzling, because all these unwanted dog activities can be cured both easily and quickly. You certainly don't need a dog behaviour expert to 'train' your dog not to chew a designer handbag if you don't repeatedly leave the dog alone in the room with the designer handbag. Nearly all dog problems are at this level of solvability. To say it's not rocket science is like describing a lettuce as not being capable of higher reasoning. So over the years I have come to realise that in many households the dog fulfils the function of being something to complain about. I don't think that's fair on the dog, particularly as I have never yet met a dog that actually wanted to be a problem to its humans. The science

Your dog may have a psycho-side, but basically you just want to be happy together.

The best of all friends: a happy, loving but independent dog.

behind this is about the dog's 'pack imperative' to survive by being acceptable to those it lives with. In practice this means that dogs are very trainable and want to be liked.

Don't beat yourself up about having got into a bit of a situation with your dog. And definitely don't worry that it's too late and nothing can be done. You and your dog will both achieve success in overcoming your problem – because you both want to. At heart, your dog wants to be a good boy, and both of you want to be happy together. You've already proved your commitment to success just by getting a book (providing you actually read it, as opposed to leaving it on the kitchen worktop where the dog will eventually chew it to pieces).

There's another important, and often overlooked, positive side to curing your dog's issue. The whole process of teaching and working with your dog is in itself very rewarding. Learning about dog problems and solving them can have a positive impact throughout your life – if you're willing to take it on board. This book will teach you how to be a psycho-dog-analyst, so that when Lassie has a problem and needs to get help, you can be there for him. However, all the best psycho-dog-analysts will analyse themselves first, and this book will ask you to be honest with yourself in answering some questions that may be hard.

For example, a great many dogs have problems in the 'social' spectrum that are not their fault at all. A psycho-dog-analyst can see that these dogs have been ignored and taken for granted, or even neglected and, very occasionally, abused. It's a great shame to discover that those dog owners who are comfortable with ignoring and neglecting the needs of their dogs sometimes behave in a similar way towards humans. So I've come to realise that dogs and humans with problems often need to get help for the same reasons. Dogs have taught me even more about humans than humans have taught me about dogs. And working with both has shown me a great deal that I needed to know about myself. So welcome your dog problem, it could be one of the best things that ever happened to you.

Now it's time for the great adventure of discovering how to build a better dog!

How to Use This Book

1 Do Nothing

This book is going to help you solve your dog problem – and soon. So it is absolutely natural that you will want to dive in with both feet, or paws in the case of your psycho dog. Stop! Do nothing! Our dogs got themselves into a canine crisis by rushing in without a plan, and sometimes we, as owners, leap in after them before we've really thought it through. However, just by bothering to read this paragraph, you've made the first step towards normalising your psycho dog. When you let yourself take a moment to think, to assess, to 'psycho-dog-analyse' the situation, you will be able to deal with the problem much more successfully than by trying to go too quickly.

But, of course, you are keen to get started, and nothing on earth is going to stop you from looking up your dog problem right now. So go ahead. Skip on to the relevant section and read it. To make things even easier, here's a quick guide to the most common problems, grouped into their behaviour categories, and showing where you will find them in *Part Two*, the problem solving section. Find the problem that relates most to you. Read the section, but promise me that you'll come straight back here when you have finished reading. If you come across multiple issues, that's a fairly strong hint just to keep reading the whole book before you do anything else.

Your Quick Psycho-Dog-Analysis Guide

1 THE ENDEARING PROBLEMS *See Part Two, p78*

● **Jumping up** – your dog constantly jumps up to put his paws on your thighs, or with larger dogs, your shoulders. The habit seems really ingrained, and he does it to your friends and even with strangers. It isn't always a problem, but when you're in smart clothes, or your friends don't like it, or there are small children around, it can become an issue.

Jumping up to put paws on your thighs isn't great when you're wearing shorts!

● **Timid** – it can be cute when your dog belly-crawls or rolls on his back or runs to hide in almost any situation, but it is often a nuisance when you want him to do something or you are going somewhere. Sometimes it also gives the wrong impression about your dog and how you look after it.

● **Possessive** – 'like a dog with a bone' is a phrase we all know, and having a dog that persistently carries a favourite toy or one of your flip-flops is usually amusing, but if he won't ever let you take it from him, or if he gets very aggressive with other people or dogs who happen to be around when he is carrying his item, you have the beginnings of a more serious problem.

● **Greed/theft** – some breeds of dog are notorious for greed, and apart from being nicknamed 'Homer Simpson' we don't take much notice. But overeating leads to more serious issues. Obesity can cause health problems, and a greedy dog may accidentally eat poisonous items, as well as inconveniently stealing food. Artful Dodger dogs that steal toys, human possessions, food, etc. are a source of amusement, until they steal items that are valuable or dangerous. Dogs don't distinguish between what it's funny to steal and what should be left alone, and owners often make the mistake of assuming dogs will somehow know that difference.

2 THE IRRITATING PROBLEMS *See Part Two, p105*

● **Pulls on lead** – among the most common of all dog problems I come across and one that escalates rapidly to a full-on out of control dog; this is a problem that shouldn't be ignored, even when it is only at the irritating stage.

● **Won't heel** – when the dog won't stay beside you if asked after he's been let off the lead.

Solo can be a bit possessive with his manky sausages toy, though really who else would want it?

● **Runs off and won't return** – this is part of the spectrum of pulling on the lead and not heeling, but more serious in its impact as it can lead to the dog being permanently lost, adopted or even stolen.

● **Won't sit or stay** – really just doesn't take a lot of notice of what the owner is asking.

3 THE SOCIAL PROBLEMS *See Part Two, p140*

● **Doesn't like me** – some owners complain their dog just doesn't seem to like them, for no particular reason. There is a reason, largely due to no bond having developed between owner and dog. Solving this issue can be very rewarding.

● **Doesn't play** – this problem is often reported by owners of rescue dogs, and some very intensively bred show or competition dogs. Luckily, teaching a dog to play is great fun for all concerned.

● **Learning difficulties** – these do arise with dogs, sometimes for health reasons, and occasionally purely because of low intelligence. They can be hard to diagnose, so it is important to be able to spot if a dog is just naughty or whether it genuinely has a learning difficulty.

● **Obsessive behaviour** – Obsessive Compulsive Disorder and repetitive behaviour very often arise where a dog is being left alone or in unsuitable surroundings for long periods of time, and requires a close examination (sometimes a self-examination) of how the dog is being cared for. They can also arise from over-training in competition dogs.

● **Barking and chewing** – is not just irritating for the dog's owner but can pose a massive issue for neighbours who have to suffer something they can do nothing about.

Constantly yapping, barking, whining and singing is also a symptom of other problems, so needs thinking about. The dog often starts chewing because it has been left alone for too long or it has been allowed to chew anything it likes. The owner should not then be surprised if the dog moves on from chewing an old trainer to chewing an expensive designer handbag.

● **Won't house-train** – is very much symptomatic of more far-reaching problems in the way the dog is being looked after by its owners, and unfortunately some owners have difficulty in coming to terms with their role in the development of this problem.

4 THE HEALTH-RELATED PROBLEMS *See Part Two, p162*

● **Weight loss/weight gain** – health issues are usually responsible, but there can be other causes and it's important to look thoroughly at the dog's way of life.

● **Appetite loss** – very often related to parasites, fever, change of routine or hormone issues. Often worrying for owners, but rarely as serious as we fear.

● **Bowel irregularity** – another problem that worries owners more than it worries the dog, but it should be carefully investigated as it can have a number of causes, one or two of which are serious.

● **Car sickness** – can usually be cured by a number of simple management measures, but some breeds are more prone, and it is a problem that is sometimes really persistent.

● **Poor coat** – all dogs usually go through periods of shedding and poor coat, but it's important to check there are no more serious causes.

● **Scratching** – usually caused by parasites and easily curable, but needs to be investigated thoroughly.

● **Head shaking** – most cases of head shaking are not serious. Often it's due to parasites, but sometimes there can be neurological and other health reasons that do need to be looked at.

● **Limping/chewing paw** – usually a very simple sign of a thorn or grass seed that has worked its way into the paw pad, but these can be very difficult to deal with and should be taken seriously. Arthritis, hairline fractures and some cancers may need to be ruled out.

● **Hyper-sexual** – there are a number of reasons for this problem and it's important to understand it fully, as simply neutering an animal may not be the whole answer.

5 THE SERIOUS PROBLEMS See Part Two, p130

● **Growling** – some breeds are more prone to growl than others, and some humans seem to like having a growling dog. However, professionals do consider it to be a problem.

● **Aggressive with dogs** – should not be tolerated, and again, it's the responsibility of the owner rather than the dog.

● **Chasing and worrying other animals** – another red-zone problem that in worst cases can lead to the criminal offence of 'livestock worrying'.

● **Bad with visitors/guarding** – far too many dog owners are in denial about this issue. It is a problem, a serious one, and it's important to admit it.

● **Biting/aggressive with humans** – many owners assume

there is a sliding scale of seriousness of biting. There isn't.
If your dog bit and no one was hurt, you just got lucky.
If the dog is aggressive with humans this is a real red-zone
problem and needs to be acknowledged, assessed and dealt
with, which may require professional help.

2 What Next?

Now you've rushed on and read the section about your dog's
particular problem, you'll be keen to know what to do next.
As the author of various dog-training and behaviour books
and a journalist who writes regularly about all types of dog;
and also as a breeder of several generations of champion
gundogs, my advice is: put the kettle on. Even if the dog's
already got the kettle, or he's eaten every tea bag in the
house, still don't start work on problem-training yet. You
could always take this book out with you to Starbucks –
leaving the dog in a safe place first.

Setting off for some training.

The great news is that nearly all dog problems are non-urgent. The dog may seem pretty psycho at present, but it almost certainly took it quite a while to get that way, and you have plenty of time to get things back to normal.

The only occasion when you may have to act swiftly is when dealing with the aggression spectrum of problems, and even in these situations it can be every bit as dangerous to rush in without thinking as it is to stand back and plan for a moment. Fortunately, dog aggression is really rare. Among some communities all over the world there is a trend for people to parade dogs from 'guarding' breeds as a kind of status symbol. It is a testament to the canine temperament globally that even among these dogs instances of real aggression are comparatively rare. Hopefully you will never encounter any genuinely dangerous dog behaviour. Even if your own dog is beginning to exhibit worryingly aggressive signs, you still have plenty of time to address the problem – especially if you do not let yourself get into denial of it.

Denial

Denial is an issue throughout the spectrum of psycho dogs, and it's something we can all be guilty of from time to time. This morning my sainted Ricky (whose role within the pack is pure and simple: the good one) attached himself to an interesting lady with two Labradors and took himself off for a walk with her. I was busy with the horses (yes, I'm a glutton for punishment) and didn't notice. Unfortunately she took a dim view of her canine guest and didn't bother to bring him back to me, instead turning him out on the main road when she arrived back at her house. Luckily the bewildered boy managed to get across the road safely and find his way back to the stables. So it was OK in the end. But, I have to admit, Ricky does have a slight tendency to attach himself to doggy strangers. This is something I have been in denial about. I got away with it this time, but I know I have to put in some training work with Ricky to remind him to stick around me even when I'm not fully concentrated on him. If I don't do something about it now, I might not be so lucky again.

Ricky realises he needs to do some revision after going off with a strange lady!

This is why your next step should be to read the whole of this book first before rushing on ahead. By the time you have finished reading, you may well realise that your seemingly trivial problem could have more serious consequences. Or you may discover that it is actually a symptom of a far deeper-reaching issue, of which you may have been in denial.

I hope too, that by reading the whole book before getting started on remedial training you will gain insights that will help you understand your dog better. The first objective of the book is to solve your problem with your dog. But the bigger aim is to stop the phrase 'psycho dog' being applicable to him or to your relationship – and there's a lot more to that than just teaching him to sit when asked. Ricky, by the way, will sit when asked for half an hour at a time, but it hasn't stopped him being nutty enough to go off with a strange lady – I bet she offered him dog drops!

Getting Started

So, having done nothing so far apart from read the book, surely it's time to do something? Well, yes, but still not very much! Before making decisions about what remedial training to do, or how to cope with your dog's psycho behaviour, you need to look at the big picture. What exactly is your dog doing wrong? How serious is the problem? How long has he been doing it? Does he do it all the time? When does he do it? And, most important of all, why? Why on earth is your psycho dog doing this?! Why did Ricky suddenly decide to go for a walk with a complete stranger?

If you are going to solve the problem successfully, you need the answers to these questions first – and they need to be the right answers. It's no good saying, 'Oh my dog's done that because he's nuts.' That much we know already.

Sometimes we even misunderstand what the dog is actually doing wrong. When people tell me that the problem with their dog is that he pulls on the lead, I ask them if the dog walks to heel. Without exception, it turns out that the dog does not walk to heel. And that is the real problem. If the dog walked to heel, he would be walking where you want him to, regardless of whether he is on the lead or not. Many people confess at this point that they rarely dare to take the dog off the lead, as he would just disappear into the middle distance. So the problem here is that the dog is not coming when called. Doesn't come when called; doesn't heel. With this disobedient dog, pulling on the lead turns out to be the least of your problems! After all, who can blame the dog for pulling on the lead if it never gets the chance to run freely? And who isn't giving it the chance to run freely? The owner. I think, if you were to ask the dog what the problem is, he might very well woof back, 'My owner hasn't bothered to teach me social instructions and now he won't give me freedom either.' All quite a long way from the original whinge that 'the psycho dog pulls on the lead the whole time'.

Sometimes the cause of a problem is much less obvious, and very perplexing for conscientious owners who have been doing everything by the book. An acquaintance has been doing everything literally by the book – my book, *From Puppy to Perfect*. He was delighted to report that after following the instructions carefully, the family's new puppy was house-trained within a matter of days. It wasn't until some weeks later that the pup suddenly began having accidents, particularly in the evenings. We chewed the problem over during a day out in the countryside, but it still took a while to realise that it was a change in the family's routine that had caused the problem. The puppy had arrived during the Christmas holidays, when my friend was around to take on the initial training. Then he went back to his work, based largely off-shore, and it wasn't until a few weeks later that he returned to the UK and a more nine-to-five pattern of commuting. We worked out that the pup, who was very much his dog, had probably missed him a bit while he was away, but the rest of the family was around. It wasn't until my friend's return that a certain amount of separation anxiety arose, exhibited by the puppy getting excited and losing toilet control when his boss returned each evening.

Apparently simple problems can be much more complex than they seem. So a period of careful observation and thinking is a good idea. On the plus side, you may also discover from your dog-watch that actually the issue just goes away when you spend more time paying attention to what the dog is up to ... something to think about!

3 Observe Your Dog

For the next couple of weeks, keep a close watch on your dog's behaviour. You'll probably need to get the family to help you with this if work and other commitments get in the way. One of the first surprising things you may notice is that the dog spends a lot more time doing his own thing than you realise. The summer that I was writing *From Puppy to*

Free-running dogs in a wide open space can still be relied on to come back when called.

Fizz posing alongside the big cup she won in her first ever competition.

Perfect, my then puppy, Fizz, was spending much of the day in an outdoor puppy run on the lawn, which happened to be right beside my study window, so I was able to watch her whenever I looked up from the computer screen (I admit, quite often). I was amazed to see what a packed schedule of completely doggy, non-human related activities she had.

First was running round the perimeter of the pen, sniffing and smelling everything. Then retreat into the shade for a quick nap. A drink of water and a widdle on waking, before getting down to the serious business of hole-digging. When the hole reached a satisfactory point, she switched to chewing and playing with her toys – tossing a ragger to one end of the run and then retrieving it was a favourite. Frequently a toy would be put in the hole, only to be removed, in order for further digging to take place. If time allowed, there was also paddling (plastic dog-bed with an inch or so of water) and sunbathing on top of the pup kennel in the style of Snoopy. There was also trying-to-climb-out-of-the-pen, a signal to me to take a screen break and come and play. So far, so psycho! Except that all these activities, and a safe, suitable environment in which to undertake them, were essential to Fizz's development. She's pictured, posing alongside the big trophy she won the following year, in her first competition.

So now it's time to get to know your dog better than you thought you did. In order to help with problem solving, you need to do this in quite a structured way, by keeping a journal of dog/family activity and any dog problems. I suggest doing it for about ten days or a fortnight, so that events that only happen weekly get included. You should note down the day of the week (and the date as well if it helps). The most important entry is obviously if your dog did its problem behaviour – e.g., dog chewed sofa; dog pulled on lead; dog chased a child in the park. But also enter any unusual behaviours or any especially good behaviours. This might include: didn't eat up; wouldn't jump into the car; sat patiently while I was on the mobile. The final column is equally important, to note down what was going on in human lives at the time. Was there anything different? Did you have a bad back and not feel like doing much walking? Were you, or a family member, especially busy with work? Were you packing to go on holiday abroad? All these kinds of factors can influence a dog's behaviour more than we realise.

Fizz enjoying life as a puppy in her outdoor play pen.

At the end of the journal, leave a space to write down any ideas or thoughts you might have had while you have been keeping the dog diary. Here's a sample of the *Dog Day Diary* I have been keeping over the last week or so. I've also added a panel for how stressful anything was, to give me an idea of the seriousness of an event, but it's not vital.

Jan's Dog Day Diary

DAY	DOG'S BEHAVIOUR	MY SITUATION	STRESS RATING
SATURDAY	Dogs pleased to see me, but quite quiet	Got back from week's skiing, knee injury, walking with stick	1/5
SUNDAY	Dogs on good form	Knee hurting, couldn't keep up with dogs	2/5
MONDAY	Dogs normal	Reduced length of dog exercise because of knee; saw orthopaedic consultant	2/5
TUESDAY	Solo came dashing in when called, and bashed my knee	Knee really sore, couldn't train dogs or walk them very far	3/5
WEDNESDAY	A friend is looking after dogs today	MRI scan, tiring and time-consuming	3/5
THURSDAY	Solo running too far away	Busy day catching up with work	2/5
FRIDAY	Solo had to be called back several times	Nothing new, waiting for appointment to get scan results	2/5

SATURDAY	Didn't do much with dogs	Quite tired with work and knee pain	2/5
SUNDAY	Dogs barked, a bit tetchy with each other, Solo not paying me much attention	Still quite tired	2/5
MONDAY	Ricky went off with a lady, took a while to find him and get him safely back	Wearing strapping on knee, helpful	4/5
TUESDAY	Exercised dogs in enclosed area, practised some training exercises	Enjoyed playing some 'old school' training games with dogs	2/5
WEDNESDAY	Dogs watching me	Have got a proper brace for my knee, so was able to do more	2/5
THURSDAY	Dogs back to normal	Did some retrieving training exercises with dogs. Still waiting for MRI results!	1/5

IDEAS/CONCLUSIONS

Things have been beginning to get out of hand, probably because of my knee injury, but I've noticed it before anything too serious has happened, and now everything is back to normal (except my knee, grrr!).

It is interesting that keeping the journal really helped me to correct a potential dog problem before it had a chance to take hold. Competition dogs like mine are always slightly borderline on the psycho-spectrum! They need to have a lot of drive and independence to be good at their work. They're generally quite intelligent too, so can get easily bored. Plus they are used to getting a lot of interaction with me, even when they are not specifically training for a competition.

So my being away for a week, combined with a change in my routine, due to my knee injury, was something that they noticed.

My knee injury definitely had an impact on the dogs' behaviour. At first they were a bit timid because I had a walking stick, which is very unusual for me. Then, as they got less exercise and training attention from me, they started playing up, especially running off – which was stressful for me. Because I was giving them less attention, they began to pay me less attention. My journal helped me notice this, so I made sure the dogs were exercised in a safe area during the period I was injured. Then I made an effort to put some extra play-training in, and this got the dogs' attention back successfully.

Even with normally well-behaved dogs, small issues can escalate rapidly. I don't often keep a *Dog Day Diary*, but looking at this one makes me realise how helpful it is in problem solving. It will be well worth your while to keep this diary when working on your dog's problem, even if it is a bit of a discipline. I've also noticed that all the more difficult problems I've had with dogs over the years have come at a time when I've been personally stressed due to external factors. This is something to keep in mind when filling in your own journal. On the page opposite is a pro forma you can print out and fill in yourself.

4 Reward and Un-reward

With a fuller diagnosis of your dog's problem and a completed *Dog Day Diary*, you're now ready to move on through the book and start the process of solving your dog's problem. This is the fun bit! Once you realise how much there is in psycho-dog-analysis, and how much can be achieved, you and your dog will be getting on fine in no time. You'll probably find yourself psycho-dog-analysing your friends' dogs, and even dogs you happen to see behaving badly around and about the place. Please don't be tempted

DAY	DOG'S BEHAVIOUR	MY SITUATION	STRESS RATING
SATURDAY			
SUNDAY			
MONDAY			
TUESDAY			
WEDNESDAY			
THURSDAY			
FRIDAY			
SATURDAY			
SUNDAY			
MONDAY			
TUESDAY			
WEDNESDAY			

IDEAS/CONCLUSIONS:

to step in and use your new knowledge. It's rarely welcome, and can occasionally land you in a heap of trouble! Instead, just be content with showing off your new normal dog.

Rewarding your dog's good behaviour is going to be a vital part of establishing that behaviour as a firm, lifelong pattern. Conversely, you will also need to know how to discourage the bad behaviour causing the problem in the first place. Specific rewards and discouragements will be discussed in each problem solving section because they may be very different according to what is appropriate for each different problem.

For example, it's counter-instinctive, but the worse the dog problem, the less you can penalise the dog. I can get away with telling off my dog for a brief outbreak of naughtiness because it is not fundamentally a bad dog. It is a good, loving dog that wants to please me, and has already been taught the difference between right and wrong – that is, between behaviour that pleases me and makes everybody happy, and things that displease me and make life difficult all round. So showing my dog I'm not pleased by some form of mild chastisement – in my case I use my voice – is more than enough to let it know to stop immediately. I've pictured a couple of my dogs immediately after I've given them a sharp 'Ach, ach'. Their body language shows how seriously they take it. Solo is lying flat and poor old Ricky is chewing his lip with anxiety. Rest assured, I gave them treats afterwards for acting so well!

If a dog hasn't been taught social skills (usually known as training or obedience) in the first place, then it shouldn't be expected to guess why you are suddenly annoyed. It won't know why it is being penalised, and the whole situation will become very upsetting for the dog (and for you too). So chastisement doesn't get you anywhere and can even result in deterioration of behaviour.

Faulty Reinforcement
For different reasons, punishment is not ideal in the case of a mischievous or even downright bad dog that knows it's

being naughty. Showing the dog you are angry or penalising it is ineffective because the bad dog doesn't basically care what you think or do. Often the dog may actually be winding you up deliberately in order to get some form of reaction out of you. By responding you are falling into the trap of faulty reinforcement, whereby the behaviours you want to stop actually get reinforced by your reactions. It might help to think of a class full of rowdy kids with an inexperienced teacher. The more wound up and furious the teacher gets, the more the merciless brats will goad the poor guy. An experienced teacher either ignores the whole thing until the kids have got bored, or better yet, attracts their full attention with something new and interesting. This is a technique you will learn to use with your problem dog. You might also want to spend some time thinking about why the dog needs to go to such lengths to get attention from you?

As an owner, you have to find ways to encourage your dog to want to please you. If you have a bond with your dog and

Solo a bit worried because I've told him off, literally rolling over.

Ricky cowering because I said 'cower' in a rough voice.

*Ginger – a
partnership
of equals.*

he respects you as a human version of a pack leader, this won't be difficult. He is a junior member of the pack, and basically has to please you, otherwise, in the wild, his days would be numbered. So you are pushing on an open door. If you show yourself to be a kind, responsible, reliable and trustworthy pack leader, then things will be fairly straightforward. We all know people in everyday life who are wonderful parents, leaders, managers and officers. This is what your dog needs you to be for him.

If things go really well, and you have the right sort of relationship, it can become a partnership of near-equals. This often happens with competition dogs or genuine working dogs such as sheepdogs. Both of you have the same objective – to win the competition or get the sheep in the pen – and you work as a team. In these cases, the work itself is often the reward the dog wants. I very rarely give my dogs food rewards. They would rather spend a day working or competing out in the field with me than any amount of Bonios (although the odd sausage at the end of the day is always very welcome all round). With your dog, you should try to discover its best reward – and be prepared to be surprised. It might not be what you imagine at all. We tend to think of food treats, but for many dogs hands-on contact or moments of wildness form a better treat. Watch the dogs finishing their run in an agility competition and you will see.

However you choose to reward, it is very important that the reward is consistent. Every time the dog does well it must be rewarded, even with just a word of praise. It doesn't matter if your knee is hurting, or things are going badly at work, the dog must always be rewarded if he deserves it. Social experiments have looked at the impact of random reward withdrawal in both humans and animals, and most have concluded that it causes personality disorders.

36

A hands-on reward, with tongues!

Equally, your reaction to bad behaviour must be consistent. I tend to call this reaction un-reward or penalisation, rather than punishment. As we look at various different psycho-situations we'll discover that old-style punishment is almost always counter-productive. The most important thing about un-reward is that you do it every single time the dog misbehaves or does its problem behaviour. If you don't bother because you're feeling happy after you had a great date last night or your daughter has got into university, then your dog knows he has got away with it and he will continue with the behaviour. When the dog pulls on the lead, most people give a few half-hearted tugs back once or twice and then give up and let the dog tow them along. So the dog has got the impression that pulling on the lead is basically OK, even though you wouldn't agree. If you stop walking and go back towards home the moment the dog starts pulling, it will soon realise that pulling is a very good way to miss out on getting anywhere. At the very beginning you may even have to put a stop to the whole walk – even when it is a lovely day and you'd like to be out on a walk with your dog!

The use of reward and un-reward throughout this book is aimed at teaching your dog, rather than simply training it. You are teaching the dog about cause and effect; about social relationships; about how to live in harmony with its community. These lessons aren't so very far different from what we need to learn to become functioning human beings. As you discover the specific techniques for each problem, remember these overall maxims:

● *Don't unintentionally reward or reinforce bad behaviour*

● *Do be utterly consistent in reward and un-reward*

● *Discover your dog's favourite reward*

● *Teach your dog before you consider un-reward*

● *Build a decent relationship with your dog*

● *Understand why your dog may be displaying attention-seeking behaviour.*

5 Coping with a Canine Crisis

There are just one or two canine behaviour moments that do constitute an emergency, where you won't have the luxury of sitting down with a cappuccino and dipping in and out of this book. These are usually medical or accident related. On rare occasions they are caused by an aggressive behaviour crisis exhibited by the dog – basically an attack or biting. Hopefully you will never encounter these situations, but in case you do, here is a step-by-step guide on how to react swiftly, safely and sensibly.

● **Step One** – Pre-save all your emergency numbers into your mobile phone, including out-of-hours numbers; it helps to have them on a speed-dial list. You will be stressed in a real emergency, and the simplest task becomes difficult. Know what equipment you might need in an emergency and where to lay your hands on it quickly.

● **Step Two** – Assess the situation. Is it a medical emergency or a behavioural emergency?

● **Step Three – Medical Emergency**
For a medical emergency, you should have a small canine first aid kit including cohesive bandages (Vetrap or similar), dropper for hydration, cotton wool, clean blanket, saline solution, Hibiscrub or similar anti-bacterial wash. Don't over-complicate your first aid kit. They are fine for minor problems, but it's more important to get the dog to a vet as quickly as possible in a real emergency. Vomiting, small cuts and lameness are not always urgent. Contact the vet immediately if your dog shows any of these signs: Loss of

consciousness; loss of heartbeat; very laboured breathing (different from normal panting); convulsions/seizures; paralysis; flickering or rolled back eyes; heavy or pulsing bleeding; pale gums; feels cold or very hot.

● Step Four – Behaviour Emergency

This happens when a dog has attacked other animals or humans; shown extreme aggression; or bitten severely. Be very wary of approaching the dog, even if children are in danger. Certainly do not attempt to 'take the dog on' in any way. The most important thing is to get the victim and yourself away from the dog and into a place of safety. If you have a companion with you, get him or her to call 999 while you are doing this. It may be possible to distract the dog in some way to give yourself a chance to remove the victim, though you won't be able to do this if the dog's jaws are closed on the victim. If you are wearing a hat, or you have a bag with you, or some similar item, toss it to one side of the dog. Some dogs have a very strong instinct to retrieve items, and this may just be enough to turn its attention from the victim. Don't throw anything that could be used to protect yourself – e.g. walking stick, gloves.

If you have a strong stick you may be able to use it to ward the dog off from the victim. Often the dog will seize the stick and start worrying that instead. If this happens, it will give you a chance to carry the victim to a safe place. Don't run away, back off slowly. If you have companions, one can distract or ward off the dog with the stick, while you carry the victim away. If you are outdoors, get inside a building and close all accesses until the emergency services arrive. If you are indoors, make sure all of you, including the victim, get out of the building and secure all doors and windows behind you so that the dog cannot get out.

The big aim in cases of dog attack is to separate you and the victim from the dog as safely as possible.

When you are anywhere near an aggressive dog, never lower your head or upper body. Use your height advantage to the maximum in order to protect your face and neck. If a dog approaches you menacingly, stand still and upright, with your feet planted in a secure bracing position. Do not speak to the dog or shout at it. Move your eye contact to a point above and behind the dog, emphasising that your eye level is much higher than the dog's, which will make you appear taller and stronger. Cross your arms in front of your upper chest. If the worst case happens and the dog does spring, your crossed arms will protect your neck and face. Very few dogs will follow through an attack when you are in this stance. The exception to this is if you are on the dog's territory, which will give him greater motivation to attack. If the dog backs down, use the opportunity to back away slowly, don't suddenly turn and run.

The above is intended for situations where the dog attack is being carried out by a strange dog. If the dog is your own dog, you should follow the same routine. However, you will be tempted to think you can reason with the dog, or perhaps even punish it. DO NOT do either of these things. DO NOT escalate the situation in any way. You must separate the dog from yourself. Depending on the severity of the dog's behaviour, you may be able to use a favourite toy, food treat or bone to lure it into a secure place like a dog pen or a room with a firmly closable door. If you can't do this, then your only option is to get everybody out of the house and leave the dog there while you call the police. If the dog is outdoors, perhaps in the garden, get away from it into a building and call the police. Make sure that no one else comes near the dog.

Never, ever leave a baby or small child alone in a room with the family dog, even if it is the sweetest-natured dog possible. Anything can happen, and a tragedy can occur from nowhere.

Your Canine Crisis Kit

● **A slip-style or chain-loop lead** – these can be looped over the dog's head with one hand without the need to bend down and get near the dog's face and mouth. You can even use a stick to put the loop in place, so there is less risk of hands being bitten. This style of lead is not cruel, and many professional dog handlers use them as their preferred training lead.

● **A strong walking stick** – hopefully there will be one by the back door or in the shed, or you can pick up a good long bit of stick when out walking. They are very useful with aggressive dogs as you can establish some control while remaining at a distance.

● **Heavy gardening gloves** – if you ever have any involvement with a potential biter or nipper these can be very helpful for protection, but don't rely on them.

● **A wire-mesh dog pen or crate** – most professional dog trainers use these in any case, but if your dog is showing signs on the spectrum of aggression or social problems, get one now, and learn how to use it.

● **A favourite food treat, preferably a large bone** – this will act as a distraction to give you vital moments when a situation is getting out of hand. Alternatively, throwing a tennis ball is sometimes enough to stimulate a dog out of an aggressive mood.

● **Welly boots** – most of us are wearing something similar when out walking dogs or in the countryside, and they do have a protective role if a dog gets aggressive.

● **Small, simple first aid kit for medical emergencies** – see above. Pre-packed kits are also available online and *Part Three* has some suggestions for where to order them. Don't be tempted by anything too technical, you're unlikely to use it and are much better off going to the vet.

A Note on Puppies:
This book is aimed at behavioural correction in adult dogs from about twelve months old.
If you are having difficulties with a puppy, this is a training issue, not a behavioural issue.

Try checking out *From Puppy to Perfect* if you are having puppy problems.

Understanding Why Problems Happen

1 Just How Nuts is Nuts?

One of my favourite Woody Allen jokes comes in the movie, *Annie Hall*. Woody's character is, of course, in psychoanalysis. Trying to delve into Woody's current relationship problems, his therapist asks: 'What about the sex? Is that OK? Do you still have much sex together?' To which Woody replies (imagine a New York accent): 'Oh God, no, hardly at all, maybe three times a week.' Meanwhile, a couple of blocks away, Woody's girlfriend is also in analysis – this is New York after all! Her therapist asks the same question: 'So how's the relationship going, are you having sex?' And she replies: 'Oh God, yes, constantly, all the time, three times a week.'

Which goes to show what very different definitions of a 'problem' we all have. What you think of as being a major problem in your dog's behaviour is something your dog almost certainly regards as just perfectly normal dog activity. My friends universally refer to my competition dogs as 'your psycho spaniels', while my fellow competitors talk about how fit they are and 'what great drive' they have (I don't think my colleagues are just being polite!). Following on from this, it becomes obvious that a dog behaviour that is acceptable out in the open countryside, or in the privacy of your garden, may not be appropriate on a city street or in a public park.

Context of the Problem

So it is important to have a good grasp of the context of your dog's behaviour problem. Terriers are well known to nip an ankle from time to time, and for many people that's not really a problem. But a nippy terrier sitting on the back of the sofa is then at head height – so your child's face becomes a biteable proposition for the naughty terrier. What was a minor problem, a nipped ankle, escalates rapidly to a serious issue: a bitten nose. Another example of this is the boisterous large dog that is a bit of a klutz. At home everybody loves the way Towser comes bounding joyfully up to you, and without even thinking of it, we brace ourselves for a full-on physical display of affection. Out in a local beauty spot, Towser spots a picnicking family and does his normal greeting-at-the-gallop and, before you know it, sandwiches have gone flying, toddlers are tearful, and parents are not seeing the funny side – which is hardly surprising.

As I write, I've just returned from a ski trip with the inevitable knee injury – both painful and unstable. After I whistled in one of my dogs, he came instantly at full speed and crashed straight into the injured knee. Suddenly, I find myself with a problem dog!

Will's Patterdale terrier, which he describes as 'a real terrier's terrier', needs an experienced owner.

> *Be aware of any of your dog's habits that could be a problem in a different context. Try to imagine how his behaviour would look from someone else's point of view.*

The Psycho Spectrum

All dogs have characteristics that are charming and endearing, particularly as puppies. How many greetings cards feature the large-eyed, floppy-eared puppy cutely dragging in someone's slipper that it has stolen? And a well-known brand of lavatory paper would never have become anything like so famous without the help of sweet little retriever pups obligingly trashing rolls and rolls of the stuff all over the house. This did happen to me in real life a couple of years ago. I'd left a pup alone for a few hours in his supposedly climb-proof pen. It wasn't climb-proof, and the loo paper turned out to be in reach as well. By the time I got back, the place looked like Glastonbury the day after. Clearing it all up was somewhat less amusing and cute than it appears on the adverts. Come to think of it, this pup grew up to be the very same young dog who crashed into my knee the other day.

As a puppy, Fizz loved carrying things around — fortunately, that's exactly what was wanted.

Behaviours that are endearing at first can eventually become problematic. This is known as the behaviour spectrum. Sometimes a behaviour that we find cute remains exactly that throughout the dog's life, and the human family adapts to accommodate the dog's foibles. Old Drake continues to carry the same manky slipper that he nicked donkey's years ago, and everybody is comfortable with it. Very often though, the dog's habit deteriorates along the scale of the behaviour spectrum to the point where it becomes really problematic. The pup that occasionally stole a sock or a pork pie, grows up to be a dog that will chew and destroy anything it can get hold of, whether it's a designer handbag or a bag of slug pellets (poisonous). Puppies that started out by sucking human fingers can grow up into dogs that bite. Dogs that are a bit disobedient escalate rapidly into being dogs that take absolutely no notice of their owners.

One of the most difficult aspects of this syndrome is that, when you are living with your dog from day to day, it is hard to notice a gradual deterioration in his behaviour until it is too late. Things slip a little bit. He gets away with one or two things. It's only when you are trying to deal with a full scale problem that you maybe look back and realise that things actually started going wrong quite a while ago.

Understand that a dog's behaviour works on a spectrum that runs all the way from endearing through tolerable to definitely problematic. The behaviour sometimes stays in the same place on the spectrum, but often escalates.

Nuts or Normal?

So when you are trying to understand why things are going wrong, it's important to start out with a good sense of what your dog's behaviour should be like: what's fine; what's tolerable; and what's definitely not OK. Use this chart to get an idea of where your dog is on the behaviour spectrum, and to what it might lead.

Nuts or Normal – rate your dog on the Psycho-Spectrum

Normal canine behaviour	Compulsive tendencies	Obsessive behaviour	NUTS!
Barks briefly when excited	Barks when greeting humans, dogs, vehicles but not for prolonged periods	Sings, howls and barks, especially at night or when left alone	Never stops barking and howling no matter what distractions
Enjoys chewing toys and bones	Will chew human's belongings – gloves, etc – if given time alone with the item	Constantly stealing items and taking them to bed to chew	Chews everything from handbags to walls
Picks up and carries small objects like sticks	Carries found items throughout a walk	Won't drop an item, returns to it constantly	Aggressively possessive about particular objects
Keen to play fetch	Pesters owner to throw fetches repeatedly	Runs repeatedly to fetch to the point of exhaustion	Runs into danger in order to fetch any random object
Runs around in circles at the start of a walk	Finds it hard to break out of circling even when called	Circles at home and in bed	Chases tail until exhausted
Can be suspicious of strange dogs	Displays fear or mild aggression with new dogs	Raised hackles, growling, ignores owner's commands	Aggressive, snarling and attempting to bite all other dogs
Likes physical contact with humans	Jumps up and paws thighs when allowed	Rather physically dominant, paws on shoulders	Hyper-sexual, false-mounting your guests
Looks forward to mealtimes	Is greedy and possessive with food and food bowl	Steals food that is easily accessible	Snatches food from hands and plates
Sometimes digs in grassy places	When left alone outside will dig several holes in the lawn	Digs inappropriately and to the exclusion of other activities	Digs in carpet, furniture, etc, until exhausted

Instinctively chases sudden movements	Chases pigeons, squirrels, etc, but stops if asked	Always chases animals and children, ignoring commands	Chases other animals and humans, worries sheep
Likes to play training games with owner	Persistently 'begs' for attention through body language	Will not allow owner to speak to other people or do household tasks	Will not rest or settle while owner is in sight
Gets briefly upset when left alone for short periods	Won't settle in its bed when left	Is destructive when left	Is aggressive with anyone trying to leave the house
Boisterous, particularly at the start of walks	Quite pushy and demanding, won't take no for an answer	Uses body contact to attract attention	Knocks over people and children
Ignores commands when something more interesting is happening	Often has to be caught and told off	Never listens to owner	Seems unaware of owner, no eye contact
Checks out interesting smells	Becomes 'deaf' when following a smell	Follows a scent for long periods, frequently returning to it	Disappears for days hunting rabbits, deer, etc
Eats weird stuff, including poo!	Won't drop 'nasties' when told to	Ignores other activities in favour of strange eating	Eats indigestible food including pebbles, soil, etc
Gets under your feet and chases you around the house	Play chews your hands and grabs your ankles	Will nip your ankles or hand, and even people who visit	Bites
Hard to get the lead on and won't walk at your pace on the lead	Pulls hard on the lead all the time	Needs to wear a more substantial halter	Pulls people over, the lead has to be let go
Is very sweet and timid	Cowers and trembles all the time	Runs off or freezes and behaves oddly	Suddenly turns nasty and bites

Case History: Dilys, Twelve Months Old

Dilys (pictured) is a female cocker-poo belonging to Anabelle. Dilys is Anabelle's first dog and Anabelle hopes to be able to take Dilys when visiting elderly people to help with therapy for problems such as dementia. Anabelle says: 'What I found really difficult when bringing Dilys up from a pup was knowing where to set the boundaries. Given what I hope to be able to do with her eventually, it was important that she didn't grow up too boisterous. I need Dilys to be the kind of dog I can take anywhere. But never having had a dog before, I didn't know how strict I should be. I took her to some training classes and that really helped. Also, I was able to respond to her natural temperament, which is really gentle and loving.'

Dilys is pictured waiting patiently in the queue for a cappuccino at Bristol's dog-friendly Boston Tea Party, so Anabelle is clearly getting things right by having an awareness that there do need to be some boundaries.

Dilys, a cocker-poo, waiting in line at Bristol's Boston Tea Party coffee shop.

2 Ruling the House Syndrome

We all have friends whose dogs rule the roost in their home. They're the friends we love getting an invitation from, but remember not wear our best Wolford sheer tights – because of their dog. Or when the time comes to go home after a lovely evening, the dog stands guard by the door and won't let you leave. Sometimes there isn't really even anywhere to sit, as large, over-friendly hounds or Labradors appear to be draped on every available chair or sofa. And, of course, there are the unmentionable sniffers, who cause everybody great embarrassment – except the dog!

These are the dogs who have really taken over, and basically want to be humans, and top humans at that. This isn't necessarily a problem in itself. Some breeds, particularly the smaller breeds, often known as 'lap dogs' or 'toy dogs', seem to manage to take charge in the most charming possible way. In the same 'ruling the roost' situation, but with a large dog temperamentally inclined to be highly motivated and even aggressive, there is a completely different picture. Play dates for the children become impossible because parents are worried about the big dog. Neighbours start to complain about constant barking. Sometimes the dog will take it upon itself to 'guard' one family member from the rest of the family, with devastating consequences.

At the very least, these dogs quickly get unruly and unmanageable, not just in the home, but when out and about. Their owners become very avoidant of taking them out in public, which just makes the problem worse. The dogs usually develop a number of problems. They may chew or generally trash a room if left alone in it for any period of time. They can be very possessive with objects, whether their own toys or items belonging to family members. Sometimes real aggression becomes an issue, to the extent where the whole family is highly stressed by the situation. At this point everybody has to face the fact that this has become a welfare issue – not just for the family, for the dog as well.

This can be very hard to accept for the owner of a house-ruling dog. Nearly always, the situation has developed through the well-meaning efforts of the owner to be kind and caring to the dog. When I suggest to owners of these dogs that the first thing they need to do is get a large indoor pen for the dog to live in, the reaction is usually: 'Oh, but we couldn't possibly do anything so cruel as to put the dog in a cage.' I get the impression they would be happier to move into a pen themselves, and surrender the house to the dog. But if things carry on the way they are, the dog may have to be given up to a rehoming centre, and if worst comes to worst, a biting incident might occur that could lead to police action.

Usually out of misguided tolerance, and occasionally out of neglect, these owners have put their dogs in an environment that has no boundaries. Any animal, or even human being, finds such a background to be very insecure. The dog that has the run of the house, in fact has no place to call its own. Everybody else in the family has his or her own private retreat – whether it's the teenager's bedroom or the dad's shed – and the dog needs the same thing. Mine have what someone once described as 'their own private wing'. Really, it's only an annexe, which they share with a load of decorating stuff! Whatever it is, a dog needs his place. It could be simply a nice, large dog-bed near his feed and water bowls, with plenty of space for him to stash his stuff – bones, raggers, socks, chews, etc. Or it could be a full-scale indoor dog kennel with his own little living area, along with bedding, favourite items, etc. In many homes, under the staircase is a good option for the dog's space, or a utility room, conservatory, hallway or corner of the sitting room.

Even as a tiny pup, Fizz already had her own puppy palace, slightly less luxurious than the one she moved into later, in case of accidents.

Having his own place gives a dog the vital sense of security he needs in order to become socialised. After all, it's hard to know your place if you don't actually have a place to know! He can retreat there if everything is getting too chaotic in the household. And it provides him with a very easily understandable boundary between what is his own special place and what is public family space, and what is private to other members of the family. This physical boundary is important in setting the tone for the social boundaries that the dog needs, both for his own mental well-being and for his interactions with humans. The dog learns rapidly that he can go and have a snooze or a chew in his place while humans are doing their own thing. Chewing and snoozing for a dog provide down time in much the same way as watching telly or dozing on the sofa does for humans. If the dog has no opportunity for down time because it feels it must constantly interact with the humans, it can quickly become overtired and stressed. Then, if the humans suddenly start ignoring it because they need to do other things, the dog is left high and dry with no alternative options.

Looked at from a dog's point of view, you can see that the 'treat him like a human' idea is in fact challenging, stressful, chaotic and random for him. Actually, there are many humans who would identify strongly with the unsettling and insecure aspects of our daily lives! Whether dog or human, we all benefit from a healthy balance between freedom and boundaries.

A dog that is constantly left to make its own decisions, come up with its own solutions and face a host of uncertainties will tend to make mistakes. Behaviourists call these 'maladaptations'. Typical maladaptations include possessiveness, aggression, territorial attitudes, dominant behaviour, displacement and compulsive activity such as barking and unwanted chewing, destructiveness, and lack of engagement with their owners. Recognise this? These are all the kinds of problems we find with our psycho dogs!

So we can understand that one of the fundamental reasons why problems happen is because of something that is going wrong in the dog's home environment. The actual psycho behaviour that we see is really only a symptom of an underlying problem that may not be at all obvious. That's one of the reasons why the first section of this book asked you to spend so much time just watching and journaling about your dog. You're going to have to do similar tasks throughout the book I'm afraid! And here's the next exercise, to find out whether your dog is ruling the roost at home.

Score	Dog Rule	v	Human Rule	Score
	Hogs the sofa, even when dirty		Puts dog in dog bed or indoor pen	
	Eats titbits from the table		Feeds dog separately, from bowl in kitchen or dog area	
	Has laddered a guest's tights		Doesn't allow dog in room when entertaining	
	Sleeps on the bed		Doesn't allow dog in bedroom	
	Sleeps in the bed		Has separate dog cushion in bedroom	
	Always has the run of the house		Doesn't allow dog upstairs or in formal rooms	
	Is aggressive with guests		Only introduces dog to guests who want to meet him	
	Steals		Removes temptation and ensures dog is not left alone for long periods	
	Won't settle while you are busy		Provides special play area and toys for dog	
	Pesters guests and family members		Sends the dog for regular down times in bed, play area or indoor pen (or outdoor kennel)	

	Won't let people leave the house	Spends time outside in play area, especially when people are arriving and leaving the house	
	Nips or bites	Has firm boundaries about dog's behaviour	
	Chews	Gives the dog purpose-made chews and toys in its play area	
	Is generally destructive when left	Does not leave the dog alone for long periods	
	Is noisy all night	Makes a regular timetable for the dog's daily activities	
	Is not house-trained	Feeds and walks the dog at regular times	
	People have commented about the house smelling	Pays attention to the dog's well-being	

For each behaviour your dog does on the pink list, he scores one goal. Score yourself a goal for each thing you do on the green list. Hopefully you'll end up with something like a score draw or you may squeak a win by a goal or two! But if your dog has won easily, then you really need to come out of denial. Your dog is the ruler in your house, and it could lead to trouble.

Case History: Violet Rose

A friend's Sealyham terrier, pictured here, is actually quite a rare breed and as such assumes it will have privileges that the family's other dogs aren't allowed. But because it is small, utterly charming and is occasionally mildly rebuked, there's no problem. Imagine a Doberman Pinscher or a large collie allowed the same access to the sofa and the outcome might be different. And yes, that really is a dog as opposed to a lovely furry pillow with black buttons!

Violet Rose is a real dog, not a cuddly toy!

3 The Psycho Tree

So the dog's psycho! That much is obvious, but the more we think about our dog's behaviour, the more it becomes clear that the dog problem is a *symptom* of stuff that's going on that we aren't really aware of – or that we might possibly be in denial about. Like when my spaniel Ricky suddenly ran off with another lady, yes it was a *problem* (as well as being very hurtful!); but it was actually a symptom of the fact that I hadn't been engaging with him very much; which was *caused* by my injured knee. The solutions to the problem then become obvious: engage with Ricky at my usual level; fix knee.

Not every dog problem is at the tip of an iceberg. Some really are just one-off, psycho situations. When you look at the problem solving sections in Part Two: The Problem Solver, you'll quickly see where your dog problem fits in. However, there are many apparently different end problems that are actually symptoms of the same root cause. So it is worth stepping away from your dog and his problem for a moment, to look at the groups of psycho behaviour. I have called each group the *Psycho Tree*. The root cause is like the roots and trunk of the tree, and the different problems arising are like the branches and leaves of the tree. Sometimes the symptom problems can seem so different that it's hard to realise they have the same underlying cause. Surely a dog that won't house-train doesn't have anything in common with a dog that is over-possessive? And yet both dogs are displaying maladaptations to their feelings of insecurity caused by stress.

Here are three sample Psycho Trees that you should find helpful in tracking down your own dog's problem.

Psycho Trees

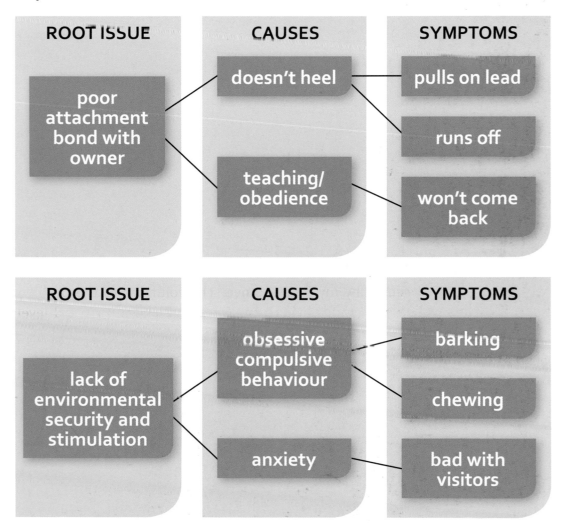

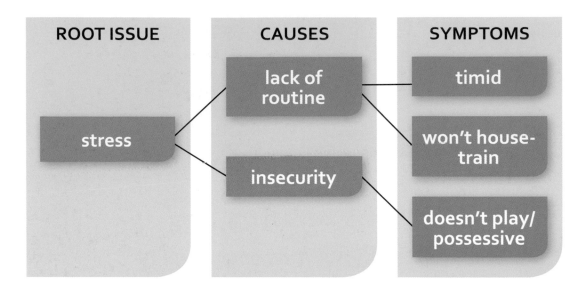

ROOT ISSUE	CAUSES	SYMPTOMS
stress	lack of routine	timid
	insecurity	won't house-train
		doesn't play/possessive

4 It's Not You – it's Me!

There's no way to sugar-coat this pill, I'm afraid, and if you've been reading so far, you may not be entirely surprised by what I'm about to write: yes, it is your fault! Or rather, having personally made most of the mistakes described in this book, I should probably say: 'It's our fault.'

When humans and dogs live together in harmony, they do so through a process of what is known as behaviour modification. Both human and dog have to change the way they would naturally do things if left to themselves. It is very far from natural to me to get up at six o'clock every morning to take the dogs out to the lavatory, stretch their legs, have breakfast, etc. However, because I enjoy having dogs in my life and I recognise my responsibility towards them, I have modified my normal behaviour (sleeping in) to adapt to their needs. The dogs have done the same. In the wild they would constantly be hunting and roaming, and scavenging food to bring back to the pack. Since domestication, my particular breed, working spaniels, has been bred selectively to highlight those attributes, along with drive, independence and intelligence. Yet when I train and compete with them, they have to control and channel these impulses in order to comply with my instructions.

In general, whether the dog is a pet or has a particular role to fulfil for its owner, the dog is called on to modify its behaviour to a far greater extent than its owner, who sometimes scarcely modifies his or her behaviour at all. I admit there are times when my sleeping-in behaviour appears to my dogs to be completely unmodified, but they are very tolerant!

Training a dog is a form of behaviour modification. We take a natural behaviour of the dog – like being obedient to the pack leader – and modify it so the dog is obedient to us and the verbal or other instructions we give it. The closer the training objective is to the dog's natural behaviour, the more successful is the training, which is why this book will help you create the right situations to solve your dog problem – pushing on an open door. Dogs are in general very trainable. Because they are social animals, the need to co-operate with those around them is hard-wired. It is much harder to train an isolated animal such as a cat. Fergus, the rescue cat, has trained me thoroughly to provide for his needs, but it is completely a one-way street. He hasn't modified his behaviours in any way that I can see, because he doesn't feel the need. Whereas dogs do get the whole concept of social interaction.

The down side of a dog's trainability is that it is just as easy to train a negative into our dogs as it is to achieve a positive. And a dog that trains easily, can just as easily be untrained. One of the biggest causes of chronic problems with dogs comes when we unintentionally reinforce an undesirable behaviour. Often it's as though we lose all common sense when dealing with our dogs. In any aspect of life, we are surely all aware, that if something you are doing is not working, then you stop doing it and try doing something else. It is this fundamental ability to solve a problem that got mankind out of the Stone Age in the first place. A Stone Age man, hitting at a piece of animal skin with a lump of rock to try to cut it, thought to himself: 'This is not working! Ug. All I'm getting is a blister.' So Stone Age man took another lump of rock and struck it against the first bit of rock until he had made a sharp edge, which he used to cut the animal skin. According to the film *One Million Years B.C.* he then used the skin to fashion a primitive bikini for Raquel Welch, and thus evolution occurred. Whatever! What Stone Age man did not do is keep hitting the skin with the blunt object.

And yet, two million years later, here we are repeatedly trying the same old failed strategies on our dogs. If it isn't working, stop doing it. As in: 'I've called and called and called him, but he's still not coming back to me.' So stop calling him and try something different. Perhaps not a sheepskin bikini, but definitely, you must try a different solution. By simply repeating the same old mistakes you are just training into your dog the very behaviour you didn't want in the first place. It's no good staying in denial and hoping that this time it will work. You have comprehensively proved that it doesn't work. Now it is time to try something different – after all, what have you got to lose?

Lots of other human behaviours end up producing problems with our dogs, and we'll discover these as we go through the book. For example, many people have trouble with their dogs being disruptive and destructive when left alone in the house – but it's our own behaviour, in going out to work and leaving the dog shut up alone for long periods of time, which has actually produced the problem. If you want to succeed in solving this kind of issue, it's important not to be in denial of your part in it. Equally, don't beat yourself up about it. Much worse things happen at sea and what really matters is doing something about it. So don't feel a desperate failure or get the guilts. So far you're maybe not brilliant with dogs. So? And of course, if you do the book, there's every chance you will become as good with dogs as with everything else.

We're all Mammals

Even top dog trainers sometimes refer to dogs as having the intelligence of a three-year-old child or being the equivalent of a toddler. This is an attempt to compare a dog's vocabulary, etc, with human intellectual powers, but actually it's very misleading. No, an adult dog is not a two or three-year-old child. It is a fully functioning adult animal. Given the opportunity, an adult dog can live happily in a social group or pack with other dogs; it can find food that it can share with the pack; it can reproduce and protect its young; it can hunt and scavenge; it has many reasoning powers; it can communicate in often complex ways; it has a full understanding of its environment. A trained dog knows how many dummies have been laid for it to retrieve and will not stop searching for the dummies until it has found them all, showing a definite awareness of quantity, if not actual numeracy.

For all mammals, including humans, these are the really important elements of survival and functioning. A lot of them are managed by the mammalian 'primitive' brain (sometimes known as the reptilian brain), and research has shown this brain area to have similar levels of development in most mammals. The frontal or neocortex is more evolved in humans, giving us additional attributes, particularly in the areas of rational processing, logic, prediction, verbalisation and dexterity. But these are in many ways just the icing on the cake of intelligence. Comparisons shouldn't make us think of our grown-up dogs as being deficient in intelligence. They are adults, just like us. If they were humans they would vote and, even as dogs, they demonstrate they can certainly have sex and go down the pub!

Many problems with adult dogs stem from owners not understanding or respecting their dog's mature and independent mind. We make the mistake of assuming our dog will continue to be as dependent on us as it was when it was a puppy or as a young child would be. But a two-year-old dog is a grown-up dog, capable of lots of independent thinking and decision-making. It has self-will (volition) and will have developed all sorts of aspirations and intentions that we as owners haven't been expecting at all. So if your dog is a grown-up male dog and there is a very attractive female dog in the area, you really shouldn't be surprised if he makes a plan to go and have sex with her at the earliest opportunity. If your dog is an adult of a sheep-herding breed, it is going to get very interested in sheep-herding if it meets any sheep – that is the family business after all.

So, as dog owners, we need to respect our dogs. You should be aware that many 'problems' are in fact natural behaviours for any adult animal. We can easily modify these behaviours through guidance and teaching so they don't remain a problem. Better still, by using our awareness, we can work with the dog to prevent the problem arising in the first place. For example, many experienced owners of working breeds recognise that their dogs will want to have a career, either in the family firm or in something that provides similar stimulation, such as obedience or agility competitions.

It's very hard to avoid anthropomorphising our dogs but, as mammals, we do have a lot in common. Avoid expecting

(Left to right)
Smell-o-vision One: *Ricky has suddenly turned and dashed in the opposite direction for no apparent reason.*

Smell-o-vision Two: *The picture as my human senses perceived it.*

Smello-o-vision Three: *My attempt to show what Ricky's senses were aware of, particularly the strong scent he was following.*

infantile behaviour from your adult dog and use your own experience as a grown-up mammal to predict where problems may crop up.

Anthropomorphism – that is, interpreting animal behaviour from a human-centric point of view – is a minefield. It is often misleading to apply anthropomorphic reasoning to dogs, and can be why their behaviour appears psycho. Supposing your dog suddenly stops and stands quivering, staring into the middle distance. As a human it is natural to look in the same direction and be absolutely baffled when there is nothing whatsoever to be seen. Then your dog suddenly zooms off like a mad thing. Psycho, surely! But the answer lies in the two very different sensory systems of humans and dogs. For a human, sight is very much our primary sense, followed up by hearing and then the rest after that. But for a dog, smell is absolutely the dominant sense, to the extent where it could be described as an extra dimension

Dog's eye view.

of which we humans know nothing. I've tried to show a few illustrations of what 'smell-o-vision' might be like for a dog. Many, many times I've seen proof of how a dog believes the evidence of its sense of smell to the exclusion of other sensory input. And the dog will be aware of things through its nose, that you are completely unable to perceive – including the presence of cancerous cells, which dogs are now routinely working to detect in medicine.

So when your dog is apparently psycho, try to use anthropomorphism in a different way. Rather than looking at the situation from a human perspective, change your point of view, and try to get into your dog's brain and 'think dog'.

Human Personality v. Canine Dogonality

One area where anthropomorphism does seem to have something to offer is on the issue of a dog's personality or character. Dogs are not humans, we know that, but if we compare one dog with another it is perfectly obvious that they do have different typical behaviours, which we can't avoid calling character. Dogs definitely have specific and unique characters! I don't think it's being overly anthropomorphic to acknowledge this; after all, the day-today evidence is undeniable. In fact, psychological research is beginning to back up this common sense observation. Crucial in the way the brain (and indeed the body) works is the relationship between that 'primitive', early part of our brain and the evolved neocortex. The structures that operate that relationship are known as the limbic system, a kind of intermediary or operating system between the older and new parts of our brain. Psychologists have discovered that the limbic system is involved in motivation, emotion, learning and memory — all attributes that we as humans would describe as character or personality.

Though they don't have such highly developed neocortices as we do, dogs certainly have a fully functioning limbic system; so it is to be expected that they have elements of personality that we can recognise and engage with as humans. But we don't want to take it too far, so throughout the book I have used the phrase 'dogonality' to describe those emotive, characterful elements of a dog's behaviour.

Gaining an understanding of your dog's 'dogonality' will help you solve much of his psycho behaviour, and you will be asked to work on this throughout the book. In fact, you may discover that what you consider completely psycho may just be a clash between your personality and your dog's dogonality. One dog owner's problem is another dog owner's desirable characteristic. My urban friends are horrified by the tendency of my dogs to get very muddy and disappear into bramble bushes, but since that's exactly what I do myself, I don't find it a problem. People sometimes worry about how 'wild' their dog is, when the animal is just exhibiting high levels of motivation that are a natural part of his dogonality.

Matching the human personality with the dog's dogonality can solve problems. If you feel absolutely overwhelmed by your dog, use the journaling techniques and thinking offered in this book to gain

Fizz has always had a lot of 'dogonality' but her full-on attitude wouldn't suit every home.

an awareness of how you and your dog fit together. It might be that your dog just isn't the right type for you. If you live in town, work in an office 24/7 and don't enjoy long country walks in all weathers, but you own a Dalmatian, that dog is going to be a problem dog for you. In which case a pug might be ideal.

5 Rescue Dogs

Estate agents say the best properties come on the market through the four Ds – Death, Divorce, Debt or Downsizing. It's a similar situation with dogs. A dog may have to be rescued or adopted for the very simple, though sad, reason that it has outlived its owner. Sometimes dog owners are forced to part with their dogs when their marriage breaks up. Or perhaps an owner may lose her job and no longer be able to afford the bills associated with her dog, particularly if it is a big dog. Or for some reason an owner has to move

He's jumping up and snatching at a bone, but just how psycho is he?

to a smaller home or perhaps a flat, where there is no space for the dog or dogs are not permitted. However, it's sad to say, death, divorce, debt and downsizing are by far the least problematic things likely to have happened to a rescue dog before becoming available for rehoming.

When a dog comes into a rescue centre or rehoming organisation it is more likely to be because something has gone really wrong. The dog may have been abandoned or mistreated. It may have been stolen and then abandoned when the thief was unable to find a buyer. A dog may have been legally removed from a home for welfare reasons. A family may have lost their dog and been unable to find it or contact whoever has found it. Now that microchipping is a requirement in the UK, this scenario should become much less likely. However, dogs that are taken into safekeeping due to genuine aggression are rarely offered for adoption, even to specialist homes.

Another frequent factor in dogs being given up for rehoming is when the family has become unable to cope with the dog's behaviour. As you will read in this book, these so-called psycho dogs are sadly so often the product of poor animal management skills on the part of the owner. I think it will be obvious by now how strongly I feel about this issue. If just one dog is saved from going into rescue by its owner reading and acting on this book, I will be so happy.

When I do occasionally breed a litter of pups, it is for myself and my friends, but a few years ago a puppy was unaccounted for. A couple contacted me and arranged to come up from London to look at the pups. I was slightly dubious, as working dogs do not generally make good London dogs, but I was persuaded that the family lived on the edge of a large dog-friendly common and there would be plenty of space, and with two young children, mum wasn't working. Alarm bells started ringing when the family turned up more than two hours late. I was envisaging desperate traffic jams on the M4 and car-sick kids, and had boiled the kettle at least three times ready to provide tea and sympathy. But no, it turned out they'd decided to stop off in Bath for lunch and sightseeing. Yes, they did have all my phone numbers.

On the front door opening, the kids charged in, kicking off their shoes and demanding to see the puppies. I took the family into the kitchen, where the litter was living. I explained that the puppies were very young still and that we should be quiet and careful. I started chatting to the parents about what they were looking for, and what kind of routines they expected to have with their pup/dog. Meanwhile, the children kept pestering to be allowed to pick up the puppies. Against my better judgement, I picked up a pup and gave it to the daughter to hold. 'Be gentle,' I was saying and showing her how to hold the puppy, when it widdled a little on her hand. Letting out an ear-splitting shriek, the child instantly let go of the puppy, yelling, 'Mummy, Mummy it weed on me!' Luckily I managed to catch the pup in mid-plummet on to the stone-flagged kitchen floor, and reunited it safely with the rest of the litter. On being informed that they would not be buying a puppy from me, the family went into meltdown: father issuing vague threats about wasted journeys; kids stomping and pouting; mum retreating into silence. Commercial dog breeders are often not so discerning about who their puppies end up with. To the estate agents' original four Ds, I would add another: Dimwit owner.

Work closely with the rehoming agency when you rescue a dog. Sometimes they will have a good background knowledge of the dog that will be very helpful. Often though, the details of the dog's past will be sketchy. Be prepared that a reputable rehoming organisation will be painstaking in matching dog and adopter, and you may have to accept that they may not consider you an experienced enough dog owner to rescue a dog with a particular issue. Most breed clubs have their own rescue section for that particular breed, and that's sometimes a good source of more or less 'problem-free' dogs that have come into rescue through particular circumstances.

Never, ever buy a rescue dog advertised on the internet with no questions asked, or with a demand that a substantial fee be paid up front. At the time of writing there is a big risk of spending a lot of money rescuing 'refugee' dogs from Eastern Europe that turn out to be dangerous or with terminal health problems. Any reputable dog rescue home or organisation will want to carry out background checks on you and meet you in your home before considering you as a possible adopter, so be prepared for a sometimes tedious process.

There's rarely a warm and cuddly reason for a dog to come into a rescue centre. In fact, if ever there was a genuine case of: 'You don't know what I've been through,' it is the story of the rescue dog. But rescue dogs can be the most rewarding and wonderful of all dogs to work with. When a dog ends up in rescue it is almost always because the Canine Contract (see *Part Three*) has broken down in some way. Usually the dog has been let down by humans. The dog's trust has been broken and it has been treated with contempt. This dog will not easily be able to trust again. So when you are addressing a problem with a dog you have rescued, always bear this in mind. Certainly, you will be able to use all the solutions in this book, but you must moderate what you do by giving the dog the additional support it needs:

● **Patience** – an absolutely vital factor in establishing a bond with any rescue animal.

● **Consistency** – the dog has been comprehensively let down in the past, and you must use total consistency to convey the message that it won't be let down again.

● **Tolerance and understanding** – based on what has gone before, your dog's behaviours may be very challenging.

● **Empathy** – it is more important than ever to get into your dog's mind and see his point of view.

When I adopted Fergus, the rescue cat, and brought him home, he emerged from his travelling box and shot straight behind the television, where he remained for the next several weeks. I was able to squeeze in a litter tray for him, along with a water bowl and feeds. He was too traumatised even to groom himself. But eventually we got there, and Fergus now stalks around the place with the same casual arrogance as any cat.

6 Dogs in Pain

When animals are in pain, their behaviour can change both suddenly and unpredictably. Pain is one of the few factors that can quickly cause a dog to escalate the situation to the point of aggression. In a dog that has not been aggressive in the past, by far the biggest reason for a sudden attack is pain. Any vet will tell you the risks of an animal biting the hand that is administering the life-saving injection. If your dog's behaviour suddenly changes or he starts doing things that are really out of character, the first possible cause you must address is pain.

Preparing to use a towel when handling an animal in pain, Lemon pretending to have a sore paw.

As you will read in the *Serious Problems* section of *Part Two*, genuine aggression is uncommon among dogs and animals generally. For them, actually biting and really

fighting is a bit like nuclear war is for us: the risks of getting into a full-scale confrontation are so great that it is to be avoided. Your dog is the same – so for him to display and then act on genuine aggression sends you a signal that something is seriously up.

Think carefully. Could your dog have been involved in an accident? Could he have been attacked by another animal? Have there been any other signs, such as loss of appetite or wanting to hide? Look at the section on *Health Problems*. Even if there is nothing obvious, and your dog continues to be unusually snappy and aggressive, it is important to get the vet to check things out.

Be very cautious when approaching a dog that might be in pain. Use one of his dog blankets or a large towel to wrap round and handle him with. If he is light enough for you to lift, use the blanket as a protection for you both while you lift. Be careful not to put pressure on internal organs while carrying the dog. If the dog is too heavy to lift, but cannot walk, get a friend to help and use the blanket as a stretcher – again, Ricky has volunteered to demonstrate this in the photographs.

Many dogs will conceal pain and injury as far as they can. This is usually because they have a high responsibility motivation. Often if you have more than one dog, they won't want to let the other dogs see they are unwell. In the wild, a subordinate dog that is obviously injured runs the risk of abandonment or even attack from within its pack. A high-ranking member of the pack has an equal imperative not to show a problem, as an opportunist from another pack might well take the chance to make a takeover attempt.

Bisto was a hyper-responsible dog and, as senior male, was my canine pack leader – the sergeant to my commanding officer. One day we were all walking on a dog friendly beach, and when everybody jumped back into the vehicle, I noticed Bisto had an enormous, rusty, deep-sea fisherman's fishhook stuck right through his lip, like a piercing. It took the vet, pliers, nippers, a file, etc, to get it out. Not once did Bisto show the slightest bit of aggression with us, even though it must have been extraordinarily painful. Lots of dogs are stoic like this, so it is easy to miss pain as a cause of a problem. Whether your dog is showing aggression or not, always be aware of injuries and health issues as a primary cause of difficulties.

7 The Ten Rules of Dog

Many professional dog trainers have a particular type (not breed) of dog they really love. It's known as the Boomerang Dog, because it keeps coming back in for retraining every summer! Common sense dictates that if a particular solution isn't working, then we try a different solution. As we have discovered, this is scientifically known as the Raquel Welch Bikini Theory. However, there is a second common sense element to this (possibly the Ursula Andress Bikini Theory) that says once you have found something that does work, don't stop doing it! And yet, where dogs are concerned, we seem unable to take these two basic propositions on board. If it doesn't work, try something else. Once it does work, keep doing it! When you stop using your successful solution, you may well find the original problem reappears – like a boomerang. To avoid this, and steal the food from the mouths of the children of professional dog trainers, follow these Ten Rules of Dog.

The Ten Rules of Dog

1 *Never Repeat Yourself – If you keep saying the same thing over and over again to your dog, he will become numb to what you are saying and start ignoring you completely. Worse still, if the dog disobeys an instruction and you just repeat it without doing anything else about it, the dog will assume that it doesn't need to take any notice of instructions. If you are sure he heard and understood what you said, then never, ever repeat an instruction your dog has disobeyed. This is the one, the only rule of dog.*

2 *Keep Calm* — Things are rarely as bad as they seem, and panicking will only make them worse. It sounds heartless, but at the end of the day, it's a dog. How bad can it really be?

3 *Watch Your Dog* — Don't expect your dog to engage with you, unless you engage with your dog. Dogs watch human body language really closely. This is where they get their reputation for being 'telepathic'. In reality they are just scrutinising and understanding our body language very carefully. By doing the same you will learn a lot about your dog, as well as being able to prevent things happening before it's too late.

4 *Keep an Open Mind* — I don't personally know that much about dogs and dog training. Everything in my books I have learnt from human experts and from dogs themselves. So if you are offered advice, give it a fair hearing, and if it's from someone you respect, follow it. If your dog is trying to tell you something, work out what that is and act on it.

5 *One Dog, One Boss* — Especially when it comes to problem solving, everybody in the family needs to be on the same page, and the fairest, most straightforward way to ensure this is to make sure only one person has responsibility for the dog. A basically good dog will get confused with lots of different bosses; a naughty dog will take advantage and play you off against each other.

6 *Go Back to Basics* — No matter how brilliantly good he was once upon a time, if your dog has gone psycho, there's a reason for it. You have to go back to square one, and keep going back, until you get to the bottom of things.

7 *Food is Your Friend* — When it comes to psycho moments, you need all the help you can get, so even if you don't normally use food treats and rewards, you can do so now. There are lots of obedience training techniques that use the food bowl and food rewards, and these are described in Part Two. You can also use food as a distraction when a dog is being aggressive. With many breeds, he who controls the food, controls the dog!

8 *Put the Lead On* – *Dogs need plenty of free exercise, but if you get a feeling things are going to go pear-shaped put the lead on while you still can, before everything gets out of hand. Remember too, that for competition dogs, the lead symbolises down time when they don't have to think about what they are doing, and this goes for many intelligent dogs.*

9 *Play Nicely* – *Whenever you are with your dog, you are the responsible adult, and that means ensuring things don't get out of hand. Wild, prolonged and uncontrolled play can exhaust a dog mentally and physically very easily. It leads to obsessive and hysterical behaviour and can become dangerous. So always keep your play reasonably sensible: planned play is preferable.*

10 *Use a Dog Whistle* – *A whistle is simple and precise, and most dogs respond to it more or less instinctively. For obedience-related problems, teaching the dog to understand a whistle is a great solution. You will find tips on how to do this in Part Two. It also looks extremely cool when your dog sits, stays, comes and turns in response to a pip or two on the whistle.*

8 How Hard Will This Be?

All dog problems are different, and some can be so minor as barely to register on the psycho scale, while others may seem worse than they really are. Keeping your *Dog Day Diary* should already be giving you a good idea of what's going on and how serious it might be. Every problem will require a certain amount of commitment from you to set it right, even if you decide to recruit the help of a professional. On the following table, score one point for each statement that applies to your situation. Generally the higher the score, the harder it will be for you and your dog.

Psycho-assessment

Behaviour descriptions

- [ ] *People have complained about the dog's behaviour*
- [ ] *I am very worried*
- [ ] *The dog has bitten/been aggressive*
- [ ] *The behaviour has gone on for a long time*
- [ ] *The dog is not very intelligent*
- [ ] *The dog is quite old*
- [ ] *The dog is rescued/adopted*
- [ ] *There doesn't seem to be much of a bond between me and the dog*
- [ ] *It isn't really my dog, though I care for it*
- [ ] *Other people in the household have different views from me about the dog*
- [ ] *I have personal or health problems*
- [ ] *My career/lifestyle is very busy*
- [ ] *It would be nice to solve the dog's problem, but I'm not that bothered really*
- [ ] *The household/daily life is very chaotic*
- [ ] *The dog is the lowest of my priorities*
- [ ] *The dog is big/from one of the guarding breed types*

None of these issues is a deal-breaker in itself, and indeed you can have ticked really any number of these boxes and still have a good chance of reforming your psycho dog. But if you have ticked a lot of the boxes regarding your personal commitment to working with dogs then you may have to be prepared to make some adjustments in your own priorities. Remember too, that generally speaking, the bigger the dog, the bigger the problem!

Having an intelligent dog with whom you already have a good bond is a tremendous positive and will make the retraining a much easier and more enjoyable process. Try these two little tests with your dog to give yourself a better idea of how intelligent and bonded he really is.

1 Basic Intelligence

Get a small edible treat out – something the dog likes, whether it might be a dog choc drop or a piece of sausage or a bit of cheese. Show it to the dog so he knows you have it. Then take a cup or bowl. Put it upside down on the floor and put the treat underneath. What does your dog do?

A Makes a beeline for the bowl and manages to get it turned over and get the treat out – *congratulations, you've got a bright, trainable dog!*

B Sniffs around a bit but can't quite get the bowl tipped back and eventually gives up – *well, he's a bit of plodder, but you should do OK.*

C Is basically completely flummoxed by the whole disappearing treat problem – *signals a dog that is really not very bright, it may be worth checking out the learning difficulties section.*

Watching me carefully, and with her head slightly to one side showing her concentration, Fizz is just as engaged with me during this training exercise as I am with her.

2 Connection

This is a useful way of finding out how the dog is really reacting to you, and what kind of a bond you have. You will discover whether he genuinely knows his name and responds to it. Let the dog play around and get a medium distance from you. If you are indoors it should be the other side of the room but not a different room. If you are outdoors, the opposite edge of a normal-size lawn is a good distance. Now call the dog, but use a completely different sounding name. So if his name is 'Bramble', call 'Coal'. Don't use any of the body language you would normally use for calling your dog, such as kneeling down, clapping your hands or patting your thighs. Just call, what does he do?

A Stops what he is doing to look at you, but doesn't come, and perhaps puts his head on one side – *a good result, the dog clearly knows what is and isn't his name, but is well bonded to you and therefore prepared to give you the benefit of the doubt.*

B Continues playing and takes no notice of you – *this is slightly worrying as the dog isn't displaying much of a bond one way or the other.*

C Comes rushing up goofily to you – *this result is typical of a soft dog who is quite needy, and you can check out some of the social issues that might be connected with his problem. Ricky has a mild version of this that we just have to work round.*

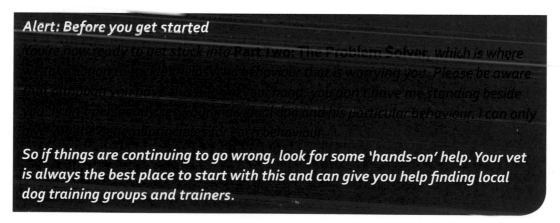

Alert: Before you get started

You're now ready to get stuck into Part Two: The Problem Solver, which is where we'll look at how to tackle the behaviour that is worrying you. Please be aware that although you have this book in your hand, you don't have me standing beside you to interpret exactly how your individual dog and his particular behaviour. I can only give you the general principles for each behaviour.

So if things are continuing to go wrong, look for some 'hands-on' help. Your vet is always the best place to start with this and can give you help finding local dog training groups and trainers.

The Problem Solver

I f you're going to be in denial of any problems, it is these cute little personality traits of your dog that you will let pass. I have to confess that my dogs jump up on me. *Oh dear!* But though these behaviours may be amusing, we have to set up boundaries for them. 'He's only playing' is fine if it's with you, at dog playtime, but it's not so good in a public place when he's just knocked over a toddler. A dog that is over-possessive of you or its toys is very close to becoming an aggressive dog. Having a greedy or a 'tea-leaf' dog makes for some amusing stories, but it's not so funny when he's being rushed to the vet after having eaten an entire giant Easter egg. We may never quite bring ourselves to put a complete stop to the naughtiness (guilty!) but we must at least realise it is an issue.

Me in full protective dog training gear with Fudge and her granddaughter, Fizz.

Jumping Up

I was discussing this question with a spaniel training friend of mine the other day as we were out with our dogs. He was wearing a smart pair of overalls, embroidered with his kennel logo, but absolutely covered in muddy paw prints. I was wearing unspeakably filthy waterproof leggings and an old coat that a bag lady would have thrown out. We both confessed to each other that our dogs jump up – well looking at us, there really wasn't much point denying it!

nigeburrphotography.co.uk

He pointed out though, in defence, that our particular dog sport discipline requires our dogs to come running straight into us, right at our feet, before reaching up to offer us whatever it is they have retrieved and are carrying in their mouths. So the normal techniques for teaching a dog not to jump up would risk our dogs being a bit reluctant or even timid about coming rushing up to us. Plus, spaniels (especially cocker spaniels) do jump up. They just do. There are various dogs and breeds of dog that are very affectionate and full-on physical about expressing it. If your dog is one of these then it is basically something you are going to have to make some choices about. I want my dogs to be really closely bonded to me, and one of the ways they do that is by exchanging physical affection. One look at Lemon and me doing twirling is enough to remind us that dogs love physical exuberance. At the same time, though, your dog jumping up on you is definitely a muddy experience. As we saw from looking at the *Psycho Spectrum*, if the dog is jumping up when you are in smart clothes or on to guests or

Me and Lemon doing twirling.

nigeburrphotography.co.uk

Just a little reminder not to jump up; as long as you are consistent, it doesn't take much.

small children, it is at the very least a nuisance, and could tip over into something worse.

How you answer the jumping up problem will depend on a number of things. How big is the dog? Obviously a big dog jumping up is literally a bigger problem than a small dog jumping up! How muddy is the dog? Again, the dirtier the dog, the more pressing the issue. What is the dog's lifestyle? If it is a working/competition dog that rarely meets anyone who is not already well-prepared to repel boarders, then it's probably not too much of an issue. But if the dog is always in the living room and meeting guests or in public spaces meeting strangers, then jumping up is a behaviour you need to discourage. And overall, how comfortable do you feel with this issue? Are you quite happy that a little nuttiness has its place from time to time? Or do you worry that things could get out of hand? Perhaps the dog has already knocked someone over? Maybe your friends have ceased to see the funny side of laddered stockings and paw prints?

Only you know the answers to these questions, and you can adjust your solutions accordingly. My spaniel training friend and I are comfortable that our dogs jumping up is part of their working activity, rather than being symptomatic of a behaviour issue. So, instead of asking the dogs to change, we've adjusted our own behaviour – certainly in terms of

Dogs waiting to finish a training session.

fashion! With my current generation of dogs (who are now conscious they mustn't show me up) I've gone a stage further by introducing a compromise solution. The dogs are allowed to jump up on me, but not on anyone else.

In some situations it is not appropriate for the dog to jump up at all. Especially with assistance dogs, you will notice that their physical behaviours are very carefully trained. As a former trustee of Hearing Dogs for Deaf People, I was always impressed that the dogs could be taught not to jump up at strangers, at the same time as deliberately using jumping up to indicate to their deaf owners if a sound had happened, for example, an alarm clock going off. Do have a look at the Hearing Dogs website, www.hearingdogs.org.uk, to find out more about this. It just goes to show what can be achieved!

For most of us, the answer to jumping up is something of a compromise. We choose to let our dogs get away with it most of the time, but if it's getting out of hand or someone complains, we try to put our foot down – with varying success! I've identified the four main different attitudes you can take to a dog that jumps up, along with the best methods to ensure the behaviour stays where you want it to be.

① Dog Should Never Jump Up

Particularly with large, heavy dogs and those with type or breed characteristics that the media like to associate with aggression, jumping up is not an option – especially if you have small children or the dog is likely to meet lots of children.

The first option for discouragement is physical action. A friend of mine used to flap his dog lightly on the nose with his tweed cap whenever it jumped up. Unfortunately the dog soon learned to catch the cap and this became an even better game, without solving the problem at all. Bear in mind also that a dog that jumps up clearly enjoys physical contact, and if you start whacking at it or pushing it down you are giving it exactly what it wants – thereby creating a reinforcement of its behaviour, which you will find discussed frequently throughout the different sections of the book.

An alternative is to make yourself much less welcoming. Do not give eye contact to the dog as it is coming for its extreme cuddle. Instead, look above and behind it. Turn your body sideways on to the dog and don't make any welcoming gestures with your hands or arms. A friend of mine is a master at sidestepping his dog's affectionate tackles, but then he did play club rugby! Some dogs will take this on board and gradually give up being so full-on, but softer dogs can be quite put off by your suddenly unloving body language. When I tested this on Ricky the other day he was devastated, and stopped in mid-rush, literally with his lower lip quivering. I couldn't bear it and we had to have massive, muddy cuddles to get over the stress of it all.

By far the most positive, and demanding, solution is to teach your dog to sit precisely. He can come rushing in to you and at the last minute you give him the sit instruction. He immediately sits still for a moment before you give him quiet reward and praise. Teaching the 'sit' instruction is described in the Irritating Problems section and in more detail in *From Puppy to Perfect* and *Training the Working Spaniel*. It is important that the praise is calm and measured, otherwise you will be rapidly back with an over-excited dog that jumps up. The first few times he gets it right, slip him a small food treat, give him a gentle rub of the head or neck and quietly tell him he's a good boy. Once the whole lesson has become ingrained, you don't need to give him a food treat. But do remember always to praise him, otherwise he will be once more jumping up to attract your attention to get his due praise.

The other important, and really rather difficult, demand of this method is the pressure it puts on you to be absolutely consistent. If you want it to work, you have to do exactly the same every time, insisting the dog sits before you praise. If you do it on days when you can be bothered or it's important because you are in smart clothes, but then you don't do it on mornings when you are rather pleased to see the dog and you are wearing manky old jeans so it doesn't matter, then you won't get anywhere with the training. The dog will always try to jump up on the off chance, and once more you end up reinforcing exactly the behaviour you don't want. Scientifically this is called 'random incentivisation' and several studies have shown how successful it is in embedding a behaviour (desirable or undesirable) in both mammals and humans. Check out the back of the book for more details.

A highly successful refinement of the sit and wait method has recently been introduced to the UK from the United States by leading spaniel trainer Ian Openshaw. Known as the 'place board' method, this uses a number of low, square table top-style platforms that the dog learns to sit on at the beginning and end of all its training exercises. The dogs take well to these because it creates a little, secure 'home territory' and makes it easy for them to relax, as well as giving a clear signal about when they are performing an exercise and when they are having a moment to regroup. I think it is the equivalent of me sitting down in front of the computer knowing it's time to concentrate, or perhaps a tennis player using the change of ends just to collect his thoughts. To find out more about place board training, check out the back of the book, go to Ian's website, www.rytexgundogs.co.uk, or watch the video on YouTube.

② Dog Shouldn't Jump Up on Strangers

In many ways this is more difficult to teach your dog than not jumping up at all because it requires you to break one of the great laws of dog training, which is consistency. How on earth is your dog meant to work out that one minute it is OK to jump up and the next it is not? And yet assistance dogs manage to take this on board. Police dogs and sniffer dogs also get the message about who they should be physical with, and in what way. Even I am beginning to achieve some success in letting my dogs know that it is OK to slime me and various dog-loving friends, but that our slightly frail neighbour finds their behaviour disconcerting to the point of alarming!

I have reached this successful compromise by being very persistent and consistent with my obedience training of come, sit and stay (which is outlined in the next section). When I see a potential target for psycho-love coming into view, I call my dogs back and sit them beside me. If it is someone I want to chat to, the idea is that they will stay sitting quietly while I am talking. This is fine if there are no other temptations or the dogs know they are in a working/competition scenario. However, if the person is someone they know or has dogs or children with them, or if it's all exciting, I take the extra precaution of putting the leads back on just to make sure. If the person is a stranger just wandering on by then I can use my whistle to ask the dogs to sit still while whoever walks by – it's not always even necessary to call the dogs all the way back to me, though it's advisable at the start of training.

A problem I have found with some of the dogs, especially Ricky, is that people seem to find them captivating. 'Oh, what a nice dog,' they say, leaning down to give Ricky a pat or a cuddle. If he happens to be carrying a training dummy or similar, they will take it from him and throw it for him, amazed and delighted when he returns it swiftly to them. They are slightly less delighted to find muddy paws embracing them, but it's too late! The damage has been done and all my teaching of Ricky has gone out of the window with a simple word of praise from a stranger.

A friend of mine has copied assistance dog organisations and had tabards made up for his dogs that have his kennel name and 'Dog in Training' printed on them. If you have to train and exercise your dog in busy areas it might be worth trying this as it does seem to help prevent misunderstandings. Ultimately the best solution is to keep your eyes open and be aware of a possible situation long before it can build up. With so many of the psycho-moments in this book, prevention is better than cure. So if you don't want your dog jumping up at strangers, do concentrate a bit when you are free exercising him so that you spot a psycho-temptation on the horizon.

③ Dogs Can Jump Up when Playing

This compromise is similar to the one above, with the important difference that it makes a very marked distinction for your dog between free exercise or play and the times when it is being taught or perhaps working or competing. If you've never attempted to train your dog before this is a good moment to think about the clear difference between work and play, and how you can help your dog to understand that. Jumping up is a great opportunity to give your dog that signal he needs. It's a bit like the bell ringing for end of school. You can see great examples of how this works when you watch dogs compete in various disciplines. During the competition the dog is absolutely serious and focussed on the boss and the job. You get the impression of a dog that has never put a paw wrong in its life, and you may even start wondering if the competition isn't perhaps a bit too strict on the dog. Then the round is completed and the dog's personality changes completely as it bounds joyfully into its owner's arms and the two of them roll round in one great furry bundle.

Picking up a tip from dog training friends, I have a special phrase I use to tell my dogs verbally that they are on free exercise, rather than about to begin a lesson. I also use it at the end of the lesson to let them know school's out. I will say: 'Go play!' or 'It's playtime!' and they know that jumping up and a general period of psycho-ness is fine. We all need to let off steam from time to time. I also have an instruction that amuses friends: 'All dogs: Run round madly!' The one command that is always instantly obeyed!

Encouraging your dog to jump up on you at the very end of a lesson is a good punctuation mark, and also reinforces the bond that you have developed during the teaching. In this way, the small problem of jumping up actually becomes a positive training tool that you can use throughout your work together.

④ Dog is Allowed to Jump Up

One person's psycho-dog is another's silly boy, and ultimately where you stand on that is up to you. If your dog is a gorgeous cute little Sealyham or a Maltese or any of those dogs that seem like a cuddly toy come to life, then the dog jumping up is the equivalent of getting a hug from a cashmere sweater. If your dog is a thick-set member of a herding/guarding breed, being jumped up on, whether enjoyable or not, can leave you feeling like you have been on a theme park ride – sort of enjoyed it, but a bit dazed and confused! Do bear in mind though, that if you are in public areas in the UK there is a great deal of legislation available to police, local councils and bystanders to control the behaviour of your dog, and you could even be prosecuted if things get out of hand. As they say: 'When the fun stops, stop.'

Dogs instantly obeying the 'all dogs run round madly' command.

The Dog Seems Very Timid

Lots of dogs, of all types and breeds, may display a range of timid behaviour that is rather endearing, but can sometimes be worrying for the owner – who is perhaps bothered that they have scared the dog or been unintentionally cruel, or too hard on the dog. Even though it may seem just a little thing, it is important all the same, to take time to think about your dog's timid behaviour and to observe it carefully. This is where your *Dog Day Diary* will be useful. Keep the journal of your dog's timid behaviour and make very careful notes about the situation in which he was timid, and what else was going on at the time. This will give an insight into the crucial question of *when* and *why* your dog seems to be timid, which in turn will help solve the problem.

The thing to realise is that not all dogs that behave timidly or appear to be timid are actually timid! The cleverest dogs can be extremely manipulative and use all sorts of tactics and behaviours to get the desired response from you. It's almost the exact opposite of jumping up – but with the same goal in mind. I think of my jumping up dogs as basically rugby players. If they've won a match, they want to show me, the boss, how thrilled they are, so obviously they all jump on top of me, pour water down my back, etc. But there are other ways of getting attention and affection from those to whom you are attached. The 'acting timid' dog wants you to love him just as much, but goes about it a different way. Think of a clever shop assistant who is out to make a sale. They may tell you that it's going to be very hard to get hold of the product you're only mildly interested in or that their manager won't let them release the item – or the classic fashion store ploy: 'There's a waiting list, I'm afraid, Madam.' They've got you then. And as soon as you decide, yes, you really want it now you've heard there's a waiting list, even though it's eye wateringly expensive and, oh, suddenly somebody's withdrawn from the waiting list. Hey presto, you can have it after all, and whoops, you've bought it, although, to be honest, you didn't want it that much in the first place.

This is essentially the behaviour of the 'acting timid' dog. When you get in from work, they may go on to their dog bed instead of rushing to greet you. So you feel guilty about having been out all day and go over to the dog with a nice treat and give it a big cuddle, and maybe another extra food treat. Or if you give your dog an instruction to stay sat, or perhaps a mild ticking off for being naughty, the dog will react as if you'd taken a stick to him. He'll belly crawl or whimper and look frightened and miserable. And you think how cruel it must have been of you to tell the dog off, even though at the time you thought you were just being quite gentle about it. The dog looks like a candidate for the RSPCA and you back down immediately.

This is known as passive aggression. It's common among humans as well and was captured brilliantly by the nineteenth century novelist Charles Dickens in his character Uriah Heep, with his catchphrase, 'I'm a 'umble man, my lord.' If you work out that your dog is just pretending to be 'umble, it's worth reading the book or watching one of the many dramatisations of *David Copperfield*, as it's quite revealing – Uriah Heep was anything but 'umble in his long-term plans and we don't want your dog having similar ideas!

The most intelligent dog I've ever had was a little black cocker called Tippy (FTCh Abbeygale May), whom a lot of people will remember. She is literally the 'grandmummy of them all' – great-, and even great-great-gran to some of my dogs. When I first started training her I just couldn't work her out. She was brilliant from the outset and learned everything very quickly, so training was easy. But often she acted as though she'd been mistreated. She was already a few months old when I bought her, so I was beginning to think bad things about her breeder or even the friend who was helping me train her. I know both people really well though, and they are top people – concerned, considerate, reliable and responsible. These are the last people in the world to be cruel to any animal. I am the same. Yet there was Tippy, cowering under the vehicle, hiding away by the back wheel, waiting to be beaten. Suddenly the penny dropped and I actually said out loud: 'Tippy, nobody has ever ill-treated or even raised a hand to you in your entire young life. You have the happiest and best life a dog could have. So get over it.'

And Tippy walked out from behind the wheel, shook herself off, and sat obediently in front of me, waiting for me to open the back of the vehicle and ask her to jump in. We understood each other. Tippy was actually a very confident dog and tremendously successful in competitions, which were her favourite form of entertainment. All her long life she never stopped trying it on, but I was wise to her. If I asked her to do something she wanted to do, like jump in the vehicle to go off training and competing, go and fetch a retrieve or sit for her feed bowl, then no problem. But give the same instructions when she didn't want to obey and it was a different story. Jumping back into the vehicle at the end of the day was impossible. It was soooo difficult and I was going to punish her for not being able to do it, and she was only a little – tiny, really – black spaniel, trying soooo hard, but soooo afraid. Even once you knew her game, it was still very difficult not to fall for it and rush over and pick her up and give her a big cuddle and let her come in the passenger footwell instead of the dog compartment – which is, of course, exactly what she wanted all the time! So here is a quick 'Timid Test' to help you find out if your dog really is timid or whether she is just a Tippy.

Take the Timid or Tippy Test

Truly Timid	Teasingly Tippy
Loses appetite under pressure	Always manages to eat up
Disturbed by loud noises	Stays relaxed when you clap your hands
Tail firmly between legs	Tail still wagging!
Rolls on back in still position	Drops shoulder and head, but rear end remains up
Freezes	Keeps on adopting different theatrical poses

	Scared of strangers	Runs straight up to any stranger – especially when in mid-cower with you!
	Backs off when you approach, even carrying a treat or toy	Immediately welcomes your approach, especially with a treat
	Salivates, chews lip	Face, jaw, lips remain relaxed
	Wets itself	Overall body and mechanisms stay under the dog's own control
	Remains nervous after the situation is over	Is instantly happy once she's got her way
	Doesn't often get involved in play	This is already a game!
	Doesn't like being picked up	Wants you to give in and come over and pick her up
	Cowers after you shout	Cowers **before** you get a chance to shout
	Shrinks from eye contact, won't hold eye contact	Loves eye contact and quite happy to stare you down

Problem: Teasingly Tippy

● This is one of those psycho-behaviours where simply understanding the problem is more than halfway to solving it. Taking the *Timid or Tippy* test makes it seem very obvious which your dog is, but you'd be surprised how easy it is to get taken in by a dog that is a clever actor. It can be quite hard to spot those telltale signs, like the fact that the dog's body language remains relaxed, even though it is giving a good impression of a refugee from the local rescue centre.

● The first cure of the problem is to let the dog know that the game is up – you know, and it needs to know you know! So definitely don't go rushing over to the dog with soothing words and arms out ready for a big cuddle. *Dog one, owner nil.*

● The next stage is much more difficult, because it will seem counter-instinctive. You should not take any measures in the way of telling off your dog, because, oddly enough, that's all part of the game as well. Even if it's in order to chastise it, you've still given the dog your full and undivided attention and, again, that's exactly what the dog wants. So in round two, the score is as before: *Dog one, owner nil.*

● So what on earth do you do? This is why it is such a clever behaviour and really I respect the dogs that are intelligent enough to manipulate me so thoroughly! Over the years I've discovered that it's rare to score an outright win in this situation. If at all possible you should just ignore the dog's manipulative behaviour. Ignore the dog. I have a tendency to say out loud: 'Yeah, whatever,' because there seems to be something in my tone of voice, and the body language I must unconsciously adopt when I say these words, that seems to be taken on board. If there is time, I just leave the drama queen to it while I get on with something else. With no audience, the dog soon stops acting. *Dog nil, owner one!*

● But on the whole, the best you can hope for is a score draw. If I'm short of time or it's not a good place for a stand-off, I just pick up the dog or drag it by the scruff or collar if it's too heavy to pick up, and put it wherever it's meant to be. If you are wanting to be doing something and it won't comply, then just put it in its basket or pen to ponder its failure. In my experience 'Tippy dogs' always want to be doing something, so the situation is much more likely to pop up when it is time to stop what you have both been doing, e.g. to go back in the vehicle. Remember to be completely neutral in your body language as you pick up or move the dog. This is a compromise situation. The dog has won a bit, because it has got attention and physical contact, but you've won a bit as well because the dog didn't get the kind of attention it wanted. *Score Draw.*

Problem: Truly Timid

If your *Dog Day Diary* and the *Timid Test* are both confirming that your dog truly is timid, then your solutions will be very different from with a Tippy dog. Where a Tippy dog actually has a lot of underlying confidence, a truly timid dog has no confidence. It will be feeling very insecure and uncertain, and it will tend to have much less conscious control over its actions than a normal dog. Truly timid dogs can often appear to be the most 'psycho' of all dogs, because their behaviour is not controlled by the same internal systems as normal-but-naughty dogs.

Where a normal-but-naughty dog is actually choosing to give your hand a nip or to run off when you call, a truly timid dog is almost unaware of what it is doing, because it is so locked into its fight or flight response. As we have seen from the *Psycho Spectrum*, endearingly timid behaviour can sometimes tip over into aggressive behaviour. Any animals, including humans, in situations they find stressful or traumatic, have four basic responses, which are triggered in the most primitive areas of the brain. These are: fight, flight, freeze and fawn.

Your endearingly timid dog is probably showing you a range of behaviours based on freezing, fawning and fleeing. So it cowers, trembles, rolls on its back or runs off with its tail between its legs. However, one day, that same timid dog may find itself in a situation so stressful to it that the fight response is triggered. I've come across cases where this has resulted in tragedy. A family with a very submissive, timid dog doesn't think twice about leaving it shut in the room with a new baby. After all, it's such a timid dog it wouldn't hurt a fly. But then the baby starts to cry – a sound that can be just as distressing for animals to hear as it is for humans. The sound of a baby crying is biologically designed to get a reaction. The dog, shut in, cannot use its flight reaction. Unseen by humans, it probably fawns and freezes for a while, which, of course, has no effect on the traumatic crying of the baby. So, with nowhere left to go, the fight reaction kicks in, and that charming dog attacks the gorgeous baby.

The dog has gone psycho, and this time it's not funny. So do forgive me for banging on throughout this book about taking even the most apparently trivial of dog problems seriously.

Looking at the *Psycho Tree*, you can see that the root causes of timid dogs are generally insecurity and stress. Although timidity fits into the Endearing Problems category when it is only mild, we do need to be aware that it can gradually get worse and, at the worrying end of the spectrum, this is very much in the group of Social Problems and even, in the worst case, **Serious Problems**. So it's a good idea to look at both of those sections to get extra help and awareness while you are following the tips given here. If your timid dog is a rescue dog, which may very well be the case, then use these measures in conjunction with the advice in *Part One*.

With a timid dog, almost more than any other of the behavioural problems, it is up to you to take responsibility. You may have to adapt your own behaviour considerably in order to allow your dog to become more confident. With rescue or timid dogs it is more important than ever to keep your side of the *Canine Contract*, described in *Part Three*. The reason your dog is truly timid is because it has been put in a situation now, today, that it finds stressful. You have to ask yourself who put it in that situation? Did it toddle out of the breeder's house on its own and open the back of your car to jump in? Did it suggest that you go out to work all day and leave it shut up, alone and lonely? Did it go online to watch bull terriers wearing studded leather harnesses? However, it will be absolutely delighted to discover that you are reading this book and so less stressful times are ahead!

Eye Contact – You can learn a huge amount, and solve a lot of problems, by becoming more aware of what kind of eye contact you have with your dog. I have shown some pictures here of various dogs giving eye contact to the boss, even as tiny pups. You will see loads of pictures of Ricky throughout this book, mainly because he is so easy to photograph! The reason he is easy to photograph is because his main joy in life is holding eye contact with me. It is so cheering to look down and notice Ricky gazing up adoringly at me. What kind of eye contact does your timid dog give you? I would expect

Eye contact from your dog is so cheering.

it's probably fairly fleeting. Don't intimidate him further by staring at him and trying to force him into giving you eye contact. Instead, wait for a good moment when the dog is relaxed and happy, perhaps enjoying a treat or playing with a toy, and briefly say his name at the same time as looking at him with a soft expression on your face. Gradually, as his trust develops and he becomes more confident, you will find he looks at you – and to you – far more often.

Routine – Just as with children, chaotic households make for stressed and unconfident dogs. So take a moment to sit down and actually write out what the dog's routine is going to be, using the knowledge you've gained from this book. Be honest with yourself about what is really going to be achievable with your routine, which might mean some compromises. It has to be something you know you can make work in the long term because, once you have planned it, you really must stick to that routine for your dog's sake. Even if you happen to be dating the hottest guy since the invention of James Bond, you have to be Cinderella and get back home in time for the dog's routine! Or at the very least recruit an understanding close friend to fill in for you in emergencies.

Security – Does your dog have a place of his own? Somewhere he can retreat to when the outside world seems very threatening? Timid dogs have a strong need for security. Just creating his own special place, with his own stuff, and letting him have down time there, can make all the difference to improving a dog's confidence. Having a castle of your own makes it a lot easier to go out from.

De-pressure – It's really important to give a timid dog the space and opportunity to be himself. Some bossy owners don't like having a timid dog and are constantly chivvying him along, trying to jolly him up and pushing him to 'get out there'. But your dog has a right to its own personality and it may always be just a bit of the quieter and more introverted sort of dog. So take a step back (literally as well) and take the pressure off. Be responsive to the dog's moods. If it doesn't like going to a certain place, then don't push it to go there. Or if it would really rather just trot along beside you instead of fetching a ball, well there are loads of dog owners who would envy you! Try to create environments and situations where your dog feels it has plenty of control and support.

Reassurance – The truly timid dog needs a lot more verbal praise and body language reassurance than tough dogs. With my more 'high drive' dogs, I sometimes feel as though one kind word from me is all it would take to tip them over the edge from mild psycho to full-on lunacy. With a timid dog it is just the opposite. When they do something they think is rather brave, you must give them loads of praise and reassurance that they have been just about the best dog there has ever been. And remember – that is brave from their point of view, not anyone else's.

Consistency – One of the quickest ways to make even a confident dog become timid is by being inconsistent; and being inconsistent with a dog that already has timid tendencies is going to make it really hard to get its trust. While writing this book I have been testing some of the techniques for dealing with various unwanted behaviours on my own dogs. This has been mildly stressful for them (thank you, dogs) because from their point of view I've suddenly done something completely unexpected and I have noticed that it has made them briefly uncertain. That's all over now and everything is back to normal, but it was striking to see how quickly my inconsistent behaviour caused a reaction in even such bouncy, over-confident idiots as my dogs. So, no matter what your mood or how hungover you are, you have to behave the same to your dog. His trying to second guess you the whole time and never knowing what sort of boss is going to turn up will prevent him from developing trust and confidence.

The Dog is Very Possessive with Food, Toys and Found Objects

Some problems are also positives! Right from earliest puppyhood, when he was the only boy in the litter, Ginger the handsome (FTCh Gournaycourt Ginger) was a great organiser. He looked out for his sisters until they moved on to new homes and at feed time he would wait until everyone had finished their feeds and then pick up all the little puppy bowls, stack them, and bring them over to me – something he still does occasionally to this day! This definitely fitted into the endearing spectrum. Apart from being both amusing and useful, this told me a lot about Ginger. I knew he would enjoy the kind of competition work my dogs do and as he matured he did indeed turn out to be consistent, capable and honest, as well as successful. However, if he hadn't been given a career those same instincts could have ended up with him being controlling, dominant and possessive. So if your dog is displaying some of these 'high drive' traits, it is well worth considering getting involved in tailored activities and training groups in your area. Check out the Kennel Club website, www.thekennelclub.org.uk, for details. In the meantime here are some tips to keep your dog in line.

● Possessive with Food

Start off by creating an environment that lets the dog know food is a privilege given to it by you, the boss. It is not something over which the dog is allowed to take control. Wherever you have been feeding the dog up until now, change it. Don't feed the dog anywhere that it might consider to be its own territory – e.g., in its pen, by its bed or in its general dog-living area. If it isn't already fed outside, I would suggest feeding the dog outside to begin with, perhaps by the back door. This is an instance where changing the feed routine can be helpful. Switch to six small meals a day, rather than just one or two big ones. Your aim is to change habits that have become entrenched. If your dog is fed only once or twice a day, hunger and the desire to eat and finish the bowl quickly will be contributing to his possessiveness over his feed. With a small feed you will soon have an empty bowl and you can practise taking it away from him. He will also get less hungry in between meals and there is the added advantage that feed time becomes less of a stand-out event.

All these small adjustments will help to break down an established pattern of behaviour, while remaining safe for you. It's important not to escalate the situation into one where you and the dog are having a battle over the bowl – and the dog is winning! Instead you are using subtle techniques

(Top)
First stage of removing a bone from a possessive dog.

(Left)
The dog shows submission and obedience.

(Right)
Everybody happy now.

nigeburrphotography.co.uk

to modify the dog's behaviour at the same time as making him feel more dependent on you.

Give these changes a chance to take effect before introducing the food bowl obedience routine described in the Irritating Problems section. One of the underlying purposes of the food bowl obedience training is to give the dog a very clear understanding that, in matters of eating, the boss giveth and the boss taketh away! This is very important for a dog as food is one of his prime motivators. Showing him that the boss controls all this raises his respect for you at all levels. You may find that solving the possessive feeding problem results in improved behaviour across the board.

As your dog adapts to the new way of doing things, you can take it a stage further, if you feel it is necessary, by teaching your dog to let you take the bowl away while it still has food in it. It's mean, I know, but if your dog has pronounced dominant tendencies it can be a useful way of just reminding him from time to time who is really in control here. By this point your dog will have fully learned the food bowl obedience routine and will sit and wait quietly near the bowl until you release him to eat. He will also be comfortable with you standing beside him while he eats.

Have a really juicy food treat in your hand. Cold sausage is my – sorry, the dogs' – favourite. After he's taken a few mouthfuls of his normal food, use the sit command at the same time as giving him the lovely sausage. Meanwhile, use your foot to slide the bowl away a little. Very likely the food treat will be even more tempting than his normal bowl meal, so you shouldn't have much trouble distracting him away from his bowl and on to you. Then praise him verbally and release him to go on eating from his feed bowl. Using your foot to move the food bowl keeps you away from any danger and gives you the opportunity to use your hands, eye contact, body language, etc. Don't overdo this exercise; just once in a while is plenty. It's asking a lot from your dog's trust and respect to take his food away from him – a bit like stealing a mate's chips without asking.

● Possessive with Toys/Chews/Found Objects

Luckily life is working with you on solving this issue: the world contains many things and he is only one dog! The more different toys and chews your dog has, the less likely it is that he will become attached to any particular one of them. So make sure your dog has plenty of stuff. We all like to have plenty of stuff and your dog is no different. If he is being particularly possessive with one toy, offer him another. Generally a dog will drop the first toy to take the second. Pick up the first toy and give it back to him. Cool! Now, by his giving you the first toy he has ended up with possession of both toys – a lesson that will not be lost on your possessive dog.

Behaviour that appears possessive to us is often caused by the dog being hyper-responsible, like Ginger with the feed bowls. If you have one or two of the dog's toys or they are spread about the place, pick them up for him and put them back on his dog bed. This way the dog can relax, safe in the knowledge that it is OK to give the boss a toy because it will end up safely back in his home.

When your dog brings you a toy or a found item and allows you take it from him, give it back to him and praise him. This is a time for a little anthropomorphic 'headology'. If you give someone a birthday present and they immediately throw it away, that's not a good feeling. Yet we do this constantly with our dogs. The conventional fetch-and-throw game that most dog owners perform all the time is basically never used by professional trainers. If your child brings you an interesting shell they have found on the beach, do you just immediately toss it aside? Of course not. You and your child look at it together for a while, as you praise your child for having found it, and thank him or her for showing it to you. Then you might give it back or your child might want you to look after it. Whatever the outcome, you have both interacted together about the shell and your bond is stronger as a result.

When your dog brings you an item and you just throw it straight away, you are enforcing a behaviour on him. He must go and get it. He found it in the first place or it is his toy, therefore he considers it his responsibility to look after it. So off he must go to get it and bring it back. And then you throw it again, and off he goes again. And again, and again. A motivated, honest, high-drive dog will never give up bringing you back that item. This means that you have inflicted a repetitive behaviour syndrome on him. In other words, you have trained your dog to have obsessive compulsive disorder. Fortunately most ordinary dogs will rapidly get fed up with the whole thing. They will get fed up with you, with the item and with everything. They will stop fetching or they will stop bringing you items, and if they do have an item they will make jolly sure they don't make the mistake of giving it to you – hence the possessiveness.

If you have a high-drive dog, particularly if he is one of the gundog breeds or types, then you are going to get brought a lot of stuff and your dog will enjoy the fetch game. But this is where you need to play that game in a creative, constructive way. Instead of throwing constantly, there are many other things you can do. You can give the item straight back to the dog or you can keep it for a while. Or, when he is not looking, you can hide it somewhere and then ask him to go and find it. All these different training/play exercises are described in *Training the Working Spaniel* and you can also find out more about them online.

My Dog is Greedy and/or Steals

These two behaviours are closely linked. A dog that steals is likely to steal food as well as other items. A dog that is greedy is certainly going to steal food if given the chance, and this will probably lead to stealing other items as well.

With a greedy dog that is not fat, immediately suspect a health issue. I'm afraid it's likely to be worms! Use your *Dog Day Diary* to be sure exactly how much your dog is eating and what. Is your current dog a larger breed than you are used to? He may need to eat more than previous dogs you have owned. And certain breeds (not naming any names,

Labrador retrievers) are just food lovers! Whether your dog appears normal weight or overweight and you are convinced it is overeating, then, armed with your diary, a visit to the vet is in order. The vet will give your dog a thorough check and advise whether he is eating too much. Most vets run doggy diet clinics and clubs, and these are usually free or just a small charge.

You may have to be honest with yourself and admit that you are co-depending in your dog's greed! Is it allowed to be at the table when humans are eating? And does it get slipped a lot of titbits? Pizzas do not exist in the wild, so your dog's digestive system isn't suitably evolved to cope with them. Regularly being able to scavenge pizzas will not only make your dog fat and farty, but it can easily lead to addiction and make him greedier than ever. The solution is in your own hands. Do not overfeed the dog. Don't feed the dog human foods or titbits. Keep food locked away where the dog cannot access it. I'm grateful that you've bought this book, but really, you don't need me to tell you how to deal with a greedy dog. All you have to do is want to deal with it, which is entirely your own decision – bearing in mind the welfare impact on your now obese, diabetic, unfit, arthritic and possibly depressed dog.

It is a similar situation with dogs that nick stuff. It tends to be something that comes naturally to retrieving/gundog types. From their point of view it is hard to tell the difference between retrieving something and stealing it – an excuse we sometimes hear in the human world! If you are around to see the dog pick up something you don't want it to, you can easily tell him to 'drop' or 'leave that'. This is part of general obedience work that is covered specifically in the Irritating Problems section of the book. Just a sharp voice and verbal ticking off is all it takes to discourage your dog from taking something. However, this does depend on two things. You have to be there in the first place in order to catch him in the act and tell him off. Plus, you have to harden your heart to how endearing it is having your dog rush into the kitchen with your husband's precious silk tie trailing from its mouth.

I do find it terribly difficult to be tough on dogs that are doing amusingly naughty things. So I always remind myself of the *Psycho Spectrum*. It's hilarious when it is your partner's mobile phone, rather than your own, that finally turns up in the dog's bed after hours of searching. But maybe it's not so funny when you're frantically looking for your car keys and already late for the school run. For me, the solution is to have important stuff well out of the dog's reach. And if I'm not around to keep an eye on the dog, I usually ask him to go into his pen for a while and play with a chew where he won't get into any trouble. Overall, the best solution I have come across in different families is to have clear boundaries between dog-friendly zones of the house and doggy no-go areas. No two families have the same zones. Some declare upstairs off-limits. Others give the dog free run downstairs except the living room. Country families with working dogs tend to keep their dogs in utility areas where there is less chance for their natural instincts to get them into trouble.

If your dog is the type of thief that actually brings his booty to you (like a retriever), don't make the mistake of telling him off. At least he's brought you the TV remote and you actually have it. If you tell him off, he might go and bury it instead next time! And there will be a next time. Dogs that steal things usually have it hard-wired into their DNA. It's really only the twenty-first century equivalent of scavenging for the pack, which they would do in the wild.

So ultimately the solution is prevention rather than cure. Use your *Dog Day Diary* for a while. This will show you what items your dog finds it most tempting to steal. You will also discover when and where he is most likely to get the opportunity to nick stuff. It can even be helpful in finding out the regular place where your dog likes to stash his swag – thus saving long searches! Throughout the book we will be discussing how we can solve many dog problems by modifying our own human behaviour, as much as by seeking to change the dog's behaviour. Dealing with theft is a good example of how we do this.

THE IRRITATING PROBLEMS

Surprisingly, it is the apparently minor problems that cause more tearing of hair among dog owners than the serious stuff, and these annoying canine behaviours are what people approach me about most of all. Given how very common they are, it's just as well that they fall into the irritating rather than the truly serious category. But before you relax too much, you should realise that these issues can escalate rapidly. A dog who pulls on the lead is a dog who wants to be in charge, which could ultimately lead to aggressive behaviour. A dog who feels free to open its mouth and bark might very well open that mouth to bite one day. Chewing a chair leg might be inappropriate and irritating for you, but eating your smart-phone is expensive and beyond annoying. Experience shows trivial mishaps with your dog can rapidly go nuclear. Plus, these problems are truly irritating!

Pulling on the Lead

This isn't going to get me any sponsorship deals with the manufacturers of dog-training equipment, but the most important thing about dealing with a dog that pulls on the lead is not to enter into a nuclear arms race of dog restraint kit. It may not actually end in mutually assured destruction, but the more halters, harnesses and what-not you put on your dog, the easier it makes it for the dog to get his full body weight into the tug of war that you are escalating. Take a moment to think of this logically. Harnesses were invented for carthorses to wear round their shoulders, to make it easier for them to pull heavily-laden carts. Like a horse, a dog's chest and torso is much stronger than his neck. So if he pulls you with just an ordinary collar and lead round his neck, that's going to go double for when he can really get stuck into it with full dog power. I saw a lady 'walking' her medium-size dog in a local park the other day. It was wearing a nose halter and lead; a collar and lead; and a harness and lead. The owner was being dragged along, I hope to the gym for some more weight training exercises as the dog had far more muscle power than her.

Hopefully though, humans generally have more brain power than dogs, which we can use in this situation. Ages ago, and very briefly, I was a truly useless novice amateur jockey. Riding even my genuine, schoolmaster racehorse was an absolute nightmare as it comprehensively got the drop on me every time we started a gallop. Then the next couple of furlongs were spent with me vainly trying to pull half a ton of equine muscle to a less terrifying speed. The trainer advised: 'It takes two to pull. Drop your hands on to its neck and you'll both relax.'

It takes two to pull; two to have an argument; two to tango ... Think about it. Your dog is only pulling if you're pulling back. Sometimes it may even be you that started the pulling – perhaps because you want to walk slower than the dog or go somewhere different from where the dog wants to go. So really, the very simple and obvious answer to: 'My dog pulls on the lead' is to do the exact opposite of what most people do, and just let go of the lead! Then for sure, the dog is not pulling on the lead any more.

Problem solved! My own dogs very rarely pull. Not because they are saints or I am a brilliant dog trainer or anything amazing. My dogs don't pull on their leads because they are almost never on the lead in the first place. The dogs generally (not always) walk or run where I ask them to, at roughly the speed I ask them to, without having to be tied to a piece of string to ensure their co-operation. But I'm very lucky. All my

dogs have been with me since they were puppies and they respect me and understand the meaning of any instructions I might give them. They have discovered over the years that I don't ask them to do stuff without a good reason, so they generally listen up when I ask them to do something.

Our other piece of great good fortune is that we live, exercise and often train quite a long way from roads or public areas. So most of the time I don't have to nag the dogs to stay close to me unless there's a necessity, such as not disturbing the wildlife. But in the UK it is actually a legal obligation for a dog to wear a collar and be on a lead when it is in a public place – so we all do have to face up to this collar and lead business at some point. Of course, the best answer by far is to train your puppy on the collar and lead from really quite a young age (about three to four months), and how to do this is described in *From Puppy to Perfect*. Once things have reached the stage where the lead is a problem with an adult dog, we need a slightly different approach.

First, you have to do the unthinkable, and just let go of the lead and see what happens. I know, there is a very real fear that chaos will instantly ensue. Most people tell me that their dog would just disappear rapidly into the middle distance if they let go the lead while it is in mid-pull. Sometimes these fears are well founded – although do take

(Left to right) Negotiating some steep steps with dogs on the lead, a time for concentration.

It can happen to anyone! The dogs suddenly see the photographer and rush to greet him.

They are definitely pulling me down these steep steps faster than I want to go!

Everything totally out of control now, time for some retraining.

nigeburrphotography.co.uk

heart because often the whole thing is far less hair-raising than we imagine it's going to be. However, just in case your most dire predictions might be fulfilled, do not let go of the lead without some careful pre-planning!

Find a medium-size enclosed space that is fairly private. The place needs to be big enough to tempt your dog to run and get it to start pulling on the lead, but it shouldn't be so big that you can't easily catch the dog if it does head for the hills. Don't use your own back garden because this is an area the dog already knows well and so won't offer it any enticement to run off. Yes, you are laying a trap for your dog! If a friend will let you borrow his or her decent-size back garden, that's great. If you have access to a local riding school, an empty training arena (indoors or outdoors) is perfect. One of my friends has permission to use the secure car park of a local industrial estate and goes to train there in the evenings after work. If you can press gang an assistant into helping you, then enclosed lanes and tow-paths are useful – plant your friend about 300 metres further along the path to catch the dog if necessary. Finding the right size area is important. Remember, big enough so there is something to tempt the dog to explore, but not big enough that it can't be caught if necessary. If you're not that athletic or a bit worried about it all, recruit a friend to stand unobtrusively in a corner as back-up should you need it. But the assistant shouldn't do anything that might distract the dog out of doing its behaviour; that is, pulling on the lead. We need the dog do the undesirable behaviour in the first place, so that we can then correct it.

STAGE ONE: The Dog Immediately Stops Pulling

Very often, and rather frustratingly, we make all these elaborate plans and get fired up for the big moment, and then the dog doesn't do anything wrong! The dog that has been pulling your arm out of its socket for the last month suddenly becomes a model of decorum, trotting along beside you as if nothing could be further from its mind than pulling.

However, once again, take a moment and look at this logically. If the dog has stopped pulling then your problem is solved. Now ask yourself why the dog has stopped pulling. The main reason is because the dog is on unfamiliar territory and no longer feels confident to start wanting to rush away from you. Also, its new surroundings are giving it so much stimulation that there is no need to pull on the lead in an effort either to get somewhere more exciting or to get to where it knows you are eventually going. If you take the dog on the same walk every day, putting it on the lead for the first ten minutes until you get somewhere where it can be allowed off the lead, then naturally the dog will want to get to the moment of freedom as quickly as possible, by pulling. Or if your walk is dull, the dog will pull due to boredom.

So if your dog doesn't pull any more when you take it somewhere new or when you change your routine in some way, that's your answer. Don't be a dull dog owner! Change your routines. Make sure the dog has plenty of stimulation on its walks and vary your walks as much as you can – even if it is only doing the normal circuit in the opposite direction. This is your solution:

> **STAGE ONE CURE: Change of Routine**

> **STAGE TWO: The Dog Follows you When Released in the Training Area**

It's hard to put an exact figure on it, but probably about 50 per cent of dogs will exhibit their pulling behaviour in the training area. So this is the moment of truth! Let the dog pull you for a few strides and then just let go of the lead, turn around and walk off determinedly in the opposite direction without even a glance over your shoulder. As far as you're concerned, that dog's history! This does take a bit of chutzpa. The first time I saw it done I was appalled, particularly as it was my own naughty dog that the trainer was washing his hands of in this comprehensive way. He just turned his back, walked off and started chatting to some people. It was as though he'd never even had a dog with him in the first place. Pretty little speckled girl cocker spaniel? Nah, don't know anything about a spaniel. I was aghast, but just as I was in the middle of imagining the most terrible outcomes that mischievous spaniel turned around and trotted back to him. Whereupon he picked up the lead and handed it to me in silence. Nuff said.

So, take courage, light the touch paper – that is, drop the lead – and walk away. After a few paces you can sneak a peek over your shoulder and see what is happening. I'm willing to bet your dog is at the very least nonplussed. He may be standing there looking at you or sniffing around on the spot, or even following after you. Let him follow or stand or whatever, but you keep walking. Change your direction of walking often and maybe even walk a few paces towards the puzzled pooch before turning on your heel and walking off again. You can even run a few paces or jump up and down. Your dog is going to be so intrigued and somewhat confused by your sudden change in behaviour that all its attention will be on you.

Getting and keeping your dog's full attention is fundamental to having a dog that works with you. One of the biggest reasons things go wrong between you and your dog is because he has ceased to notice your presence or even because he never really noticed you in the first place. I use a dog whistle to give complex instructions to my dogs – but I only ever use that whistle if I genuinely have something I wish to communicate with them. So instead of it being some kind of constant white noise in the background, it is a noticeable event. You and your dog having a constant tugging battle with the lead rapidly becomes something to which he is numb. Your dog is probably barely even aware of something that you are finding a big problem. So suddenly

Once your dog's attention is really focussed on you, she won't pull on the lead.

changing your behaviour, thus breaking the habitual pattern, is going to get his attention. There is lots more about this throughout the book, especially in *Part One: Understanding Why Problems Happen*, and also in the Social Problems section. It is worth revisiting that information, but first let's put the final touches to solving the pulling on the lead.

If you've got him at least mildly intrigued, it's quite likely that he'll quickly join in this game of grandmother's footsteps. This is the time to let him catch up with you. Without breaking your stride, quietly pick up the lead and keep walking about as before. Keep the lead as slack as possible the whole time. If you find it is getting taught, then make your change of direction briefly in the opposite way (you may find yourself pulling him for a moment), then back in towards the dog, which will automatically give you some slack. It also means the dog will have to make some changes of direction, backwards or sideways, that he has to think about, and that have definitely been initiated by you.

Do all this just for the minimum amount of time it takes to get results. Follow your instinct. You will know when you are making progress. If the dog starts pulling again, drop the lead again. Don't ask too much at this stage. Even if it has

An on-lead exercise of heel, sit, heel, sit – note the slack in the lead and the dog sitting quietly waiting to heel again.

only taken five minutes, that's fine. If you go on too long you could end up substituting one habit for another, so keep it short and sweet. As soon as you have got the change of behaviour, finish the lesson and give your dog a reward.

Think in advance about what reward you will give. I suggest keeping your dog's favourite toy in your pocket and giving it to him as soon as he has been good on the lead. Once he discovers his favourite toy lives in the boss's pocket, pulling on the lead is going to be yesterday's news! If your dog doesn't have a favourite toy, I advise you to look at the Social Problems section. Many dog trainers use food treats and clickers with this kind of work, but I find it all a bit of a faff. Ultimately I want to get to the stage where my dog loves me, not a mechanical device. One of the rewards my dogs really enjoy is being allowed to snuffle their noses up my coat cuffs until their entire muzzle disappears up my sleeve – I fear it is because I am smelly ...

A dog that joins in rapidly with the grandmother's footsteps game is demonstrating a connection with you, which is great news. In this case the lead pulling is likely to be little more than a bad habit the two of you have just gradually developed. Keep repeating the lesson from time to time, especially if the dog starts pulling again. After the first couple of lessons you won't need to go through the stage of dropping the lead. Just do the maze-walking – turning away from your dog (your turn to tug on the lead if necessary) and turning back into the dog (to give you back slack on the lead). The good news is that you can do this anywhere and you'll probably find other dog owners queuing up to learn the trick.

> **STAGE TWO CURE: Adopt New Behaviours to Break an Ingrained Habit**

> **STAGE THREE: Dog Races Off when Released in the Training Area, but Returns when Called**

This is the thing dog owners fear the most! Sometimes when searching for a dog you get some helpful workman shouting over: 'Cheer up, love, it may never happen!' Just before throttling him, I would mention that it has happened already. The dog has run off. It has happened to me many times and usually when I was unprepared for it, so the dog really has had the opportunity to disappear over the horizon. But over the years, it's all been OK in the end. Here we all are and the current generation of dogs have benefitted from my often scarring experiences with their predecessors, so we all chunter along happily enough.

Now, when your dog runs off you can at least profit from my occasionally harrowing mistakes. For a start, you are prepared for the dog to run off and you've made sure it can't get that far, and may even have a friend around to help with catching if necessary. And the other massive positive is that you are going to learn a lot about your dog just by letting it run off.

Firstly, call it back. Does it come straight back, looking a bit sheepish? That's great news. It shows us that your dog is not an out-and-out hoodlum. He clearly listens to you (from time to time anyway) and is basically co-operative. You and your dog are just going to need a bit of a refresher course on heeling and obedience, which is covered under the *Won't Heel* heading coming next.

> **STAGE THREE CURE: Call Dog back and Practise Basic Obedience Work**

STAGE FOUR: Dog Runs Off and Ignores you

If you have called your dog back and you might as well have been talking to yourself, at all costs **do not repeat** your call back instruction. I'm afraid I'm repeating the *'do not repeat an instruction'* instruction throughout this book. So, be warned, this is the last time in this section that I will give you this precious, most important of all, piece of advice. Instead I will just explain why it is so important. If you keep saying the same thing over and over again, like I'm just saying the same thing over and over again, as I have repeatedly kept writing the same thing over and over again, how long do you keep reading? Or paying attention?

It is the same with your dog. If you just keep on yelling his name, his name, his name, it rapidly becomes completely meaningless. It's certainly not something of which your dog feels the need to take any notice. There was a wonderful Cockney comedian who used to complain about his wife's chatter: 'Somefing buzzin' in my ear ...' he would say. I'm afraid you are well on your way to becoming just background noise as far as your dog is concerned. And then what if you say: 'Come here! Dazzer, come!' and by some miracle he actually does notice you've commanded that, and he also understands what you're asking, and then he doesn't do it? If you then don't do anything, except stand there and keep saying, with increasing desperation: 'Dazzer, there's a good boy! Come here, lad! Come! Dazzer! Good lad, come!' how much respect is your dog going to have for that line of attack?

You will say, as everybody says to me every time: 'Oh, but I never do that.' But you do! You may not realise you are doing it, but your dog certainly does. I have actually gone so far as to record on my mobile people pleading with their dogs to come back. I recorded this from a middle-aged, very successful, professional man: 'Teal, come! Come here, Teal. Teal! Good boy. Come! There's a good boy, Teal! Come!' It left me wondering what it was that was so 'good' about Teal (names changed to protect the innocent!).

114

So if you're not just going to stand there yelling yourself hoarse after having let go the lead, what are you going to do? This is where the pre-planning comes in. Because it is an enclosed area, carefully selected, you don't need to panic too much, because things can't go that far wrong. If you're reasonably athletic and sharp off the mark you can quickly get after your dog and grab hold of the lead or put your foot on it, so you can catch him again. Do make sure you choose ground you can easily run on. I was doing this on a Highland moor one day and tripped headlong over a heather root. I had my whistle between my teeth as I was running, but luckily the peat was so soft I didn't do myself any injury. My friends were doubled up with laughter: 'You were so cross,' they giggled, 'You were up and running again in a trice, you hardly missed a beat!'

Yes, very funny, but we don't want it happening to you, so do be sure of your footing. An alternative is to recruit your friend to hide or be as inconspicuous as possible, in roughly the area the dog is likely to run. Then, when it runs off and ignores you, your friend can jump out suddenly and grab the lead. This will surprise your dog considerably – and possibly even make it think twice about repeating its bad behaviour!

The main thing about this stage of the exercise is that you have discovered your dog does run off and that it ignores you. However, you have also caught it successfully and are now in a position to plan your next step. The exercise has shown very clearly that the problem you have with your dog is not that he is pulling on the lead. That is just a symptom of your real problem with the dog, which is that he is disobedient. His pulling on the lead is because he genuinely is trying to run off, as opposed to the behaviour exhibited by dogs in the other stages of the exercise, which are just pulling out of habit, confusion or boredom, or even because you are pulling them. So you should move on to the next

Lemon has quickly obeyed the sit/stay command even though I'm not holding the lead, but it's trailing there just in case I need to tread on it.

problems – **Won't Heel** and **Won't Return**.

These issues take rather more teaching time to solve than the simple issue of pulling on the lead. While you are teaching the dog, he will need exercise and lavatory facilities as usual. If you still have access to your safe, enclosed area, use that and spend as much time as possible playing with the dog with it off the lead. Also, use the area for the teaching exercises to come. Remember to poop scoop thoroughly. When you and the dog are out and about in public places, a flexi-lead will give him a bit more freedom and you can keep adjusting it to try to avoid too much pulling. I'm not generally a huge fan of flexi-leads (partly because of my own incompetence in getting them constantly tangled up), but this is one time when they have a role.

> **STAGE FOUR CURE: Use Safe Exercise Techniques While Commencing Obedience Teaching**

The Dog Won't Heel

The various dog problems of pulling, not heeling, running off and not coming back are all so connected up together that it is difficult to write about them individually. However, it is important to recognise them as separate problems because that is how they register with harassed dog owners. If the first thought of the novice dog owner whose dog pulls on the lead is: 'Oh, yes, heeling issue here, must remember to do some revision of heeling patterns tomorrow' then nobody has a problem. There would be no psycho dogs to write about! How wonderful if we all had such presence of mind and common sense. Well, I didn't have it when I started with dogs and neither did my friends. When our dogs pulled, we tugged back. This was occasionally very comical. One of my friends had a big, handsome dog, with the emphasis on big. His girlfriend was very slight but walking the dog was her domain and sometimes we would see her in full cartoon mode, being towed along so vigorously that her feet actually left the ground. If only the dog had been reminded to heel.

Outside of the various competitive disciplines, I almost never see a dog that heels. When people complain to me about their dog pulling on the lead, my first question is whether or not he heels. Mainly people are convinced the dog does heel. So far so good. Now, while the dog is on the lead, ask him to heel. If he does heel, that is what he will do and obviously he will stop pulling the lead. This makes sense doesn't it? If the dog is walking to heel beside your leg, he can't actually pull the lead can he? Not unless you have such a short lead he is actually hanging off it. After years and years of suffering, this all seems so obvious now. If the dog is pulling, just say heel. And if you have taught it to heel, there you are.

Of course, there is a massive 'if' here. The elephant in the room – or on the lead – is that the majority of dogs don't, won't or can't heel. And if they are lovely family pets who are going spend their lives skipping around, playing and being cuddled, what's the point of them heeling? After all, we can just put them on the lead when we need to, can't we? And what happens when you put them on the lead? Just mentioning ...

Puppies that are going to compete in various disciplines when they grow up are taught to heel quite young. Most dogs that have any kind of job to do, especially assistance dogs, are also taught to heel. The Kennel Club recommends that well-socialised dogs, whether pets or not, are able to heel. Your vet probably hosts all sorts of dog training and socialisation classes.

If you want to cure, or better yet, avoid, a mound of the problems described in this book, getting your dog to walk quietly alongside you is a massive help. Think of it in human terms. If you're out for a walk with a friend, you tend to walk alongside each other because it's more friendly; you can chat and generally interact with each other. With your young children, you always make sure they know there are times when they have to walk alongside Mum and Dad, and perhaps hold hands if it's a busy place. It's the same with your dog. There are times when you and he want to 'chat' with each other through body language and other interaction, so being close beside each other is important. And there are times when it is a busy area when you need to make sure your dog is safely alongside you, probably on the lead as well as heeling.

Attentive heeling is a wonderful tool for bonding between you and your dog. Lots of you will have seen 'dancing dogs' and heel-work to music, where the fulfilling mutual communication between dog and handler is obvious. I'm not suggesting your dog needs to be an accomplished professional. My own dogs are a bit rough and ready, but they need to be very attentive to me for their competition work in the field. So I am often doing heeling refresher exercises. I will have my dog off the lead, heeling alongside me, and then, with the smallest of commands, I will ask the dog to sit while I carry on walking, without breaking my stride. Usually I use just a small, flat-palm hand gesture at my side or I might pip the whistle just once, or just say quietly 'sit' or 'hup'. The thing is to keep walking without breaking your stride in any way. The dog should instantly sit as instructed and stay watching while you walk away. You can turn and walk back to him. As you are beside him, you just say 'heel' and pat your palm against your thigh and continue walking without breaking your stride. The dog will immediately get up and start heeling alongside you. There are a load of variations of this exercise – and it can become a bit of a party piece for a pet dog! You can see this kind of exercise performed in competitions on YouTube.

These exercises are all part of the general bond of mutual connection/obedience that we will discuss later in the section. First though, it's time to test where your dog is now on his heeling. So off to the secure area and let's ask the dog to perform the exercise I've just described. Never mind, I couldn't do it either to begin with! It has taken years of help from wonderful professional colleagues, who know so much about teaching their dogs, to understand why these exercises work and how to teach them to your dog. Most dogs pick them up quite quickly – and get a buzz out of them – so let's get started.

STAGE ONE: Dog Can't Heel

Most of the dogs I see not heeling aren't being disobedient, they just don't know about heeling because they've never been taught. If your dog came into the household as an adult – perhaps a rescue dog – then obviously you can't be held responsible for his not knowing how to heel. And for some reason it's one of those things we all take for granted that a dog will automatically know how to do. Perhaps it's because of all those well trained dogs on the telly or because we so often see the older, calmer type of dog pottering along contentedly alongside his owner, we just tend to assume that all dogs heel. From personal, sometimes very personal, experience, I can inform you that not all dogs heel naturally! Certain breeds and types of dogs are never really comfortable heeling. The working breeds and those very driven to follow scents find walking to heel quite a tedious chore. They would rather be out there, getting stuck into it, whatever 'it' turns out to be, and who knows what 'it' might be until you've got stuck into 'it'? This is what my dogs emote to me. However, once I've taught them how to heel, they will certainly co-operate, although they do find long heeling sessions quite stressful and demanding.

First of all check whether your dog knows how to heel. Put him on the lead. I usually use a 'slip' or loop lead when training. It's much easier to take it on and off when necessary than clipping on leads or getting collars done up. Have your dog on the lead as you walk along in your training area. Say: 'heel' at the same time as slapping your thigh with your hand. Obviously this should be the dog-side thigh! Most trainers have the dog on their left-hand side, but it doesn't really matter and if you've got several dogs you'll probably end up with them heeling on both sides of you. As you give the instruction, quietly let go of the lead and continue walking for a few strides. Then take a sharp 90 degree turn in towards the dog and keep walking. Do this again after a few strides and again until you have basically walked a square.

Even the very first time a lot of dogs will trot alongside you quite happily. They don't have that much choice because they are on the inside line of the square you are walking, so you tend to be between them and anywhere else to go. After you have walked the square, as quietly and as unnoticeably as possible, pick up the lead and continue walking on in a straight line for a little further. Lead the dog in a gentle circle in the opposite direction – we don't want dizzy dogs and owners at this crucial stage. Now repeat the original exercise, remembering 'heel' and thigh-pat as you drop the lead and walk the square. After you've walked the square, pick the lead up quietly and walk on a bit. That's enough for now. Don't make a huge fuss of your dog and give him big praise. The idea is that he doesn't notice the difference between being on the lead or off the lead, but he does learn that 'heel' means following in close.

The next lesson is to be walking some more complicated shapes. Have your dog on the lead and walk forward about ten paces before turning sharp right, then walk another few paces before turning left. Then randomly continue walking around the place, sometimes turning back on yourself completely or walking a circle. While you are walking these patterns, from time to time give your 'heel' commands and drop the lead before picking it up again after a short while. Most dogs will concentrate on you and stay beside you simply because they don't know what you are going to do next. Some more enterprising dogs will quickly distinguish between being on the lead and more or less off the lead, and will try to take advantage. In this case it is easy just to tread on the lead and bring the dog up short, re-instilling that vital element of doubt about whether you have actually got physical control over him or not!

If you find that your dog responds to this quite well, then it's very likely that his heeling issue has been that he just has never really been taught how to do it or got the message. A friend of mine whom I much admire and is one of the best spaniel trainers in the country once told me that all this close obedience work, such as heeling, is just kidology. His dogs follow his instructions at distances of 500 metres away and that's a bond, not kidology. But at the beginning of teaching, the two things are much the same.

> **STAGE ONE CURE: Teach the Dog how to Follow at your Heel**

> **STAGE TWO: Dog Won't Heel**

Here's a test to see how your dog is thinking. Put the dog on the lead as before, giving the lead plenty of slack. Now give your 'heel' command and signal, but don't let go of the lead. Just keeping walking along in a straight line. If he obediently follows close to your heel, not pulling on the lead, it's an indicator that he does know the meaning of the command. Now repeat the command and keep walking, but this time drop the lead. Don't give your dog the benefit of the doubt by walking squares as you did before. Just go on walking in a straight line. If the dog continues to trot alongside you with no difference between you holding and not holding the lead, great! He probably both understands the instruction and is willing to co operate with it, at least initially. Your problems may have been down to perhaps forgetting to give the command clearly and correctly; or other obedience and social issues that we'll look at later.

For now though, the main thing is that he has co-operated with the instruction and is heeling. Don't push it too long, just quietly pick your lead up and end the exercise. This is an occasion for reward. Why? Because the dog has changed his behaviour. Before, he disobeyed the instruction to heel (on or off the lead), and now he has obeyed it. So we want positive reinforcement for that – such as something to sniff, eat or play with or a cuddle or verbal praise.

Now comes the real test – will your dog continue to co-operate when he is off the lead completely? Have the dog on the lead as usual to start with. Give your heel commands and quietly lean down and take the lead off completely, continuing to walk forward as you do so. I'm afraid this is usually the moment when the lessons that had been going so well suddenly turn a bit pear-shaped! Even the dimmer dog knows instantly that the lead is no longer on, and this is the moment of truth. If he immediately shoots off, then your issue is most likely to be down to disobedience rather than lack of understanding. If, by any miracle, he continues to heel then walk a square with him before putting the lead back on and ending the exercise with praise. It's likely that you've just had your wires crossed somewhere along the line and you both need to pay some attention to revision training along the lines discussed, before moving on to the more detailed obedience work described below.

Remember, it's as easy to untrain a dog as it is to train it. If you've fallen into slack habits of letting your dog get away with things, you will have to do revision from time to time. This is another of those deep-rooted issues that give rise to a lot of different dog problems, so check it out in *Part One*.

If your dog does run off, catch him and put the lead back on quietly without either praising or telling off. You and the dog have a bit more work to do. Heeling is all about the degree of attachment – bonding – between you and your dog. Dear old Lemon, currently the senior lady of the pack, is beginning to get on a bit and I find these days she comes and walks along with me even when everybody is on free play. I guess we've both slowed down a bit!

Where bonding hasn't quite got firm yet, remember my friend's kidology method. I've watched him and I can't quite put my finger on how he does it! He certainly doesn't use food treats. But mainly it seems to be just the sheer force of his personality. He gives the dog a lot of eye contact and he chats to it a bit (nonsense mainly), and he moves his hands and flicks his fingers. And, of course, he keeps changing direction. Overall, the impression I get is that he's very engaged with the dog – he's concentrating on it and what they are doing together. It seems to make him very charismatic to the dog, so that it finds him more interesting than anything else around, and ends up heeling out of general curiosity. It's a valuable lesson: if you're not interested in your dog, why should your dog be interested in you?

My version of kidology is to have my dog's favourite toy in my hand. Oddly enough, this frequently happens to be an old pair of my socks, knotted together. I'd rather not think about what this says about my socks – it works, that's all that matters. I can wave the sock bundle about a bit and tease him a little with it just to kid him along and keep him interested in being by my leg. Occasionally I give him the toy as a reward for heeling. This is one of the occasions where you could also use a food treat, held in your hand, as an encouragement and reward. Slap your thigh occasionally to hold his attention. Remember to change direction all the time in order to keep him guessing. If you are lucky enough

Solo with a bundle of old socks that I keep in my pocket or my hand to give him as a reward for heeling, and to keep him interested in me.

to have a very narrow green lane or alley near where you live, this can also be a good place for training heelwork. The lane will be too narrow for the dog to go anywhere except alongside your leg, and if he does try to make a dash ahead it is simple for you to reach down and put your hand in front of his nose to let him know he can't go forward.

It is easy to forget that heeling is part of obedience for your dog and something he has to make an effort to do, just as much as any of the other exercises we teach him. A lot of people have their dogs on heel and then forget about it, leaving the dog having to concentrate quite hard for a long period of time while the boss is just wandering along enjoying a country walk or chatting to friends. This is very often where the problem of not heeling has started in the first place. So if you are not going to be concentrating on your dog for a while for any reason, put him back on the lead so that he can relax and know he doesn't have to think about anything while you're chatting with your next door neighbour or admiring the roses.

STAGE TWO CURE: Practise Heeling Exercises

The Dog Won't Return

Maybe I'm biased towards seeing the good in all dogs, and I do admit there are some real delinquents out there, but my feeling about dogs that won't come is that they *would* come – if they thought you really meant it. By far the most common reason I find for dogs not coming back when called is that they have been trained not to return. And guess who's trained them not to return? It's us! Usually it is the dog's own boss, or possibly other members of the family, who have trained their dog not to return. Obviously we don't do this deliberately or even notice ourselves doing it – but it is down to us. There isn't some evil dog trainer from the dark side who comes every night and takes the dog out for midnight disobedience sessions!

There are many ways in which we train our dogs not to follow instructions. Sometimes there is faulty reinforcement, where we unconsciously punish the dog for doing the right thing or reward it for doing something bad. Or we just don't bother to communicate effectively with the dog. By doing this, we teach the dog that there is no real talk between us. Dogs can easily learn a human vocabulary of around thirty words – but only if we bother to teach them those words in the first place. The French think the English are terribly rude because we never bother to speak to them in French. It is hilarious to watch English dads on French holidays asking a Frenchman for something in English – usually tomato ketchup – and bellowing the same words louder and louder, 'tomaaato ketchup!' until the deafened Frenchman shrugs his shoulders and walks away.

Do you remember when you first got the dog? For most of us it was probably an adorable little bundle of puppy that we brought into the house. At that age it learned its name very quickly. When you said, 'Fizz!' it would come toddling across the kitchen, falling over its paws, in an effort to come to you and play. In those days you could say, 'Fizz, come!' and Fizz would be there as fast as her chubby little legs could carry her. Not just in the kitchen or sitting room either; out in the garden there was never a problem in calling Fizz to you to come and play or to come back indoors for dinner. I have only ever had one puppy that didn't automatically come when called and that was Toffee, who genuinely had mild brain damage, and I will be writing about his problem in the Social Problems section. So the vast majority of adult dogs who don't come have at some point learned not to come. How did this happen? Where did it all go wrong?

STAGE ONE: Boundary Testing

I think there's probably a biological imperative for all young animals to test the boundaries at some point. They have to discover what their place in the world is going to be. Will they be leaders, constantly discovering new things and allowing others to follow on? Will they be brave heroes, capable of achieving wonderful feats? Or maybe they will be followers or more timid types, content to let others go on ahead.

If your dog is a youngster who has only just started not coming back when called it's very likely he is still testing his boundaries. That's great, well done for noticing now while it's much easier to do something about it. Because of their competition breeding, my dogs' attitude to boundaries is basically, it must be admitted, contemptuous! So as they grow up I am constantly checking to see how far they are pushing the envelope and whether it is time to check them back a bit. This is a hard line to tread because when they are grown-up dogs they are going to have to be brave soldiers, diving into the depths of bramble bushes where even the boss would fear to tread. You get used to your young dog's dogonality though, and soon learn how tough or not to be.

Some puppies and young dogs don't come back because they are feeling confused or timid and you need to be able to pick up these signals. When Solo was growing up he didn't obey his 'come' instruction one day. Here we go, I thought, and instantly switched on The Voice. You know the one I mean! We humans use it on each other all the time. It means: end of messing around or there will be dire consequences. 'Ach, ach, Solo!!' I thundered. Whereupon, poor Solo instantly threw himself down on the ground and showed me his tummy. Unlike all the rest of the family, he wasn't a very brave pup, perhaps because he'd been hand-reared, so there was no way he was risking coming back to the boss. Luckily I realised from his body language that he was nervous rather than naughty. So I got down on my knees and opened my arms and said in a welcoming, soothing voice: 'Solo, lad, come here ...' and he was immediately with me.

In families I occasionally find a cause of tension that a young dog will come back to all members of the family except the dad – who, of course, considers this to be a major insult. A lot of the time though, it's purely because, as the only adult male in the house, the dad may be a bit full-on for the young dog. Of course, the opposite can also happen. My ex-husband had to cope with so many different dog incidents during our marriage that the dogs and I have dedicated this book to him! One story he tells is a perfect example of adult dogs testing boundaries. He was walking my champion, Lyn, one day when a rabbit jumped up not far away from them. Even he can see the funny side of watching Lyn looking first at the rabbit and then at him, measuring the different distances. He says you could quite clearly see her thought process: 'Is deputy non-executive pack leader going to be quick enough to get to me before I can get to that rabbit? No way! Yippee!' And off she went in chase of the rabbit. Boundary established, and broken!

As your dog's boss, the idea is never to let the dog realise that it is in a position to break a boundary and get away with it. The most important thing is to notice immediately when your dog hasn't followed your instruction to come back. Maybe give him the benefit of the doubt if it is the first time and he is still quite young. It can really help with this if you make sure you always ask the dog to come at a moment when his attention is on you. If you ask him to come when he has just seen an amazing bird or next door's cat you are up against some fierce competition! But if you ask him to come when nothing much else is happening, and perhaps he is already looking at you, then you are pushing on an open door. If you happen also to be holding his feed bowl for dinner or waving his favourite toy then you are stacking things in your favour. Don't let it enter his head not to come; we want to get the dog to get into the mental habit of 'oh, yes, come. I always come when I hear that'.

With an older dog or one that you have already given the benefit of the doubt you will have to be stronger in reminding it that there are boundaries and that you are the person who defines those boundaries. You need to be quite careful how you do this otherwise you could end up unintentionally reinforcing the behaviour you don't want, as described below. The younger the dog and the more recent the problem, the more likely you are to be successful with some simple 'come' revision exercises. Always start from this point in any case, just to make sure your dog really has learned and understood about 'coming'.

Use an enclosed area for your revision training; it doesn't have to be that big. As long as your dog is learning that when it hears 'come' it always stops what it's doing and comes back to you, it really doesn't matter how far. Even just a few yards is sufficient to establish the command. Nor do you want the dog too far away in case you have to run out to him and establish a physical contact.

Let the dog play around a bit. Choose a moment when there's not much else going on and hopefully his attention is already somewhat on you. Say clearly, in a neutral tone of voice: 'Fizz! Come!' At the same time jog backwards away from him for a few strides, bringing his chase instinct into play. You can wave his toy and chuck it in the air or you can do the exercise at feed time and be holding his food bowl. If this works, great! Just repeat the exercise regularly, but gradually reduce the number of additional incentives to the point where you can just shout: 'Fizz! Come!' and your dog will come immediately without you doing anything else. Gradually add in more temptations for him to disobey you; for example, calling at a moment when he is distracted with something else.

Don't do the exercise too often, just two or three times a day is plenty. It is really important to give him a big reward when he comes to you, even if there has been a little bit of a slow burn. A really physical, affectionate cuddle, combined with very nice, encouraging voice praise is the best reward long term. At the beginning, if you've been using feed times, toy or whatever, then getting the food or the toy is the reward. But ultimately what you want is a dog that comes to you, not the dinner you are providing. This may sound familiar! So the quicker you can get to a reward that is based on bonding and attachment between the dog and you, the better established your contact will be.

If your dog is naughty from the start, and won't come even if you are waving a feed bowl around or if he starts disobeying again after a period of clearly understanding what you want, then he really is testing you out – and you must step up to the mark! Use The Voice, to say 'Ach, ach, bad!' but remember not to repeat the command. He heard you. Some dog owners have a lot of difficulty modulating their voice when talking to dogs. Some people find it really hard to get sufficiently sharp tone, while others tend to overuse tough talk. Practise using both and be able to switch from one to the other instantly, as soon as the dog's behaviour changes. Dogs are really responsive to tone of voice. I think we all know people who really couldn't say 'boo' to a goose, and we hear them gently telling off their dogs 'baaad little boy' in a way that the dog is clearly finding very soothing. If this is a problem for you, then think of something that has really annoyed you recently and let rip! But the second the dog has responded, switch back to nice cop.

Often The Voice will be enough, but if you're not great at The Voice, or the dog has been getting away with boundary breaking for a long time, you are going to have to get physically involved. Dogs are responsive to tone of voice and, a step up from this, they have the utmost respect for physical body language! The moment your dog disobeys your Voice, walk up to him sharply, grab him and drag him towards you, while saying 'come'. No need to be nasty about it, just firm. If you are bothered that your dog will bite you, may be aggressive or turn on you in any way when you do this then you have a much deeper problem than a dog that won't come. It's time for you to look at the **Serious Problems** section. While you are researching those issues then you should exercise the dog on a flexi-lead until you are more confident to be able to revisit this obedience work.

> ## STAGE ONE CURE: Re-teaching and Revising the 'Come' Instruction

> ## STAGE TWO: Faulty Reinforcement Issues

One of the big mistakes many novice dog owners make is to wait until the dog has finally come back and then tell it off for running off or not coming back earlier. Think logically about this. If you tell it off when it comes back, you are effectively telling it off for coming back, i.e. for obeying the instruction. So you are punishing the good behaviour you wanted to teach in the first place – you see what I mean about how we unintentionally train disobedience into our dogs. On the whole, dogs are not stupid. If a dog thinks it is going to get punished when it comes back, then it's definitely going to think twice about coming back!

So, even if it has been quite a palaver getting the dog to come back, when it eventually does return like a prodigal son remember to reward it as described above. This does leave a conundrum though, of how to let the dog know clearly about its bad behaviour and avoid reinforcing that bad behaviour. I remember puzzling over this after reading the first dog training book I ever bought. The book advised rattling a rolled up newspaper over the head of a disobedient dog. In the middle of the North Downs, with a dog that liked to be naughty at a distance from me of at least 100 metres, I have to tell you, this piece of advice was a complete non-starter.

This is why I have spent so much time in this section discussing how to prepare for your corrective training work. Essentially you have to set things up in such a way that when your dog does his bad behaviour, you are already at an advantage – if you like, you can say you have picked the battlefield! If your dog does his bad behaviour where you aren't really in a position to do anything about it, then you just have to catch him (with help if necessary) and chalk it up to experience until such a time as you are better placed to do something about it along the lines described in this chapter.

In the meantime, it's important not to reinforce his bad behaviour. Don't plead with him to come back. Dogs should beg to humans, not the other way round! Don't use a nice voice or a particularly nasty voice. It's often best not to say anything at all. Catch him, put him on the lead and take him straight home. Don't let the dog know that you are rattled by his behaviour, even if you are absolutely hopping mad. Some dogs will take advantage of your harassed body language and get a kick out of winding you up. Their disobedience will get worse and worse, egged on by your reactions. They are pressing your buttons and effectively being rewarded by knowing that they are in charge of your behaviour, rather than the other way round. Some time ago, scientists were doing some experiments with dolphins to see how they reacted to various external stimuli and associated rewards. At first the scientists were absolutely baffled by the very inconsistent results of their experiment – until they realised the dolphins were deliberately 'faking' their results to see how the scientists reacted! 'Only messing,' emoted the dolphins. Make sure your dog doesn't get the chance to do the same thing.

One of the main ways we fault reinforce – that is, train disobedience into our dogs – is the same way we train our children to behave badly. As long the dog (or child) is playing nicely, we ignore it. The dog may come up to us voluntarily to seek reassurance that it is doing the right thing, but because nothing has gone wrong we barely notice the dog trying to attract our attention. The only time the dog gets our full concentration is when it's doing something we don't want it to. So the dog very rapidly learns a range of behaviours guaranteed to get some sort of interaction or stimulus from us. Obviously, one of the most common of these is not coming when called.

No matter what, whenever the dog turns up at your feet extend a friendly hand and recognise his initiation of communication. If he brings you something unspeakably disgusting, thank him for it – allow him to keep it if you possibly can, the last thing you want is to be carrying a cow pat around for the rest of the walk – but thank him nicely all the same! Even if you're very busy with something else, acknowledge your dog and then suggest something he can do (perhaps in his dog spot) while you are busy. When I'm writing, my dogs are usually in their outside pens playing or quite often just ignoring each other. If they are in the study with me, the constant overtures of pairs of damp, doggy paws on my jeans make writing even tougher.

> **STAGE TWO CURE: Acknowledge and Praise Good Behaviour Rather than Reacting Only to Bad Behaviour**

STAGE THREE: 'Numbness' to Return Instruction

Most of the time, the issue of dogs not coming can easily be overcome with revision of general obedience training. It's also very important that we, as owners, adapt our behaviour so that we don't keep making the same mistakes and falling back into old habits. Sometimes, though, the problem of not coming when called can become really ingrained. The dog has heard and ignored the verbal command 'come' so often that the word will never now hold any meaning for it.

There is also an issue with high-drive dogs from the various working breeds: gundog and hound breeds are very responsive to smell. In all dogs the sense of smell is by far the most highly developed of a dog's senses. It will believe what it smells far more than anything it may see or hear. As human beings, the world of scent is very largely closed to us. Apart from roast food and, for some bizarre reason, grapefruit, humans don't have a very good sense of smell at all. But for dogs, smell is like a whole extra dimension of which we have no concept. When your dog suddenly goes haring off into the middle distance, it is very likely be lured by a particular smell. If the smell is strong and interesting enough, all the dog's other senses get pushed to one side. I've seen a dog run straight into a wall in these circumstances.

For these reasons, a dog really can become quite numb to the call of 'come'. This is where the whistle comes in. If you have unfortunately taught your dog over the years that the word 'come' is meaningless or if he has a great tendency to follow his nose, teaching him to return to the sound of a whistle can rescue the situation. It is a completely new command, so he won't have become numb to it, and a whistle has sharpness to penetrate a dog's brain even when a smell is monopolising it. So by teaching the dog the whistle, you have a chance to start all over again – and get it right this time!

There is no need to get a fancy 'silent' whistle, a stag's horn or anything like that. For ordinary training the basic 'Acme' plastic whistle is fine. Check out the back of the book for whistles and where to buy them. There are three basic whistle commands: 'come', 'stop' and 'turn around'. In combination, these three commands mean that you can control exactly what your dog does and where he goes, even at a considerable distance. If you have ever watched sheepdog trialling competitions you will probably have marvelled at the extraordinary way the shepherds can move their collies so precisely from such a long distance away, but if you listen carefully, you will find they are using combinations of very simple commands that any of us can teach our dogs.

These are the whistle commands I use:

● 'Pip' repeatedly for about three to five pips means 'come'.

● One long 'peeeeep' means 'stop' and I expect a fully trained dog not just to stop but to sit up and look at me to see what we are going to do next.

● 'Pip' twice gently means turn around and go in the other direction. Many people never use this third command, but if you do get interested in various dog training activities it comes in useful.

Ricky after the 'stop' whistle, watching and waiting for the next whistle command.

The 'Come' Whistle

For now, all you need to do is teach the 'come' whistle, but if you are interested, you can learn the other two as well. If you get very interested in all this, you could check out *Training the Working Spaniel*.

Start out by seeing how your dog responds to the whistle. While he is playing around in the garden, wait until a moment comes when his attention is more or less on you. As usual, waving a toy is a good way of getting attention. Have the whistle already in your mouth and blow: pip, pip, pip, pip. I usually

blow three to four pips. No more. You don't want him getting as numb to the whistle as he is to the verbal 'come' command. If you are lucky, your surprised dog will look up and come running over to you to see what's going on. Give him a big reward! Cuddles, toy, food treat, whatever it takes for him to know that this is very special. The pip, pip, pipping of the whistle means amazingness!

I've found that this surprisingly instant reaction happens much more often than you'd imagine – particularly if you choose your moment carefully, when the dog hasn't got much else going on anyway. There's no point blowing the whistle if another family member is already playing with him. Remember, always look for doors that are at least half open when you are trying to modify your dog's behaviour.

If it works the first time, don't be tempted to overdo it. Leave it at that for the day. At present the element of surprise is working with you and you don't want to lose that. But repeat once a day in the garden for a couple of days. Always give a good reward and you will soon have the dog bounding up responsively when it hears the whistle. But this is just over a short distance, on home territory.

Now it's time to move to the training ground that you have used for previous exercises. Get the dog attentive by doing some of the lead and heeling work described above. Don't make a big meal of it. Just try to get a feel that you and your dog are connected and working together. Now take your dog off the lead and let him have a roam around as you did in the garden. Pick your moment and pip your return whistle. At this stage I also like to give plenty of body language encouragement to make it really welcoming for the dog to come zooming back for treats and cuddles. Get down low and spread your arms out. If he comes straight in, wonderful; lots of praise and treats. Then let him go off for another little roam around before quietly walking up to him and slipping the lead back on to end the exercise.

You don't want your dog to get the idea that the moment he comes back to you it means the end of play. A lot of people are so relieved when they finally recapture their dog or he eventually returns that for the dog it's wham, bam, lead on, back in the car, end of fun. Instead, returning to you should be the beginning of pleasure for the dog, not the end of it.

If the dog doesn't come to the whistle as he was doing in the garden, then just take your training back a stage and do some more work in the garden. No panic, just patience! If he does get it right first time, don't be tempted to do it again 'just to make sure'. If your teenager gets an A* in her exam, you don't ask her to do it again, just to be sure – what an insult! Do practise your whistle 'come' for a few days after, looking for one successful performance each time. If you overuse the command, you will end up making the dog numb to it, just as you did with the verbal command.

From this point forward you can incorporate the whistle into your daily life with the dog. But please don't repeat your mistakes! If the dog doesn't come to the whistle, do not keep blowing the whistle. Take action along the lines we have discussed already. The use of the whistle instead of the verbal command had basically given you a second chance with your 'numb' dog; please don't ruin it. There is a big tendency among dogs and humans to let things slide. 80 per cent is good enough, and then 50 or 60 per cent is OK, and then before you know it, things actually aren't really happening at all. If you let it slip now, it will get worse! So, patiently insist that your dog does exactly what you want at the precise moment you ask him to. If that's not happening, then backtrack and start again from where things started to go off course a bit.

If your dog ends up deaf to both verbal and whistle commands, it doesn't leave you with anywhere to go. 'Oh yes,' said an acquaintance, airily. 'You can always use an electric collar.' But if someone has already let their dog get numb to two different forms of command, it's not a big step for them to get the dog numb to a mild electric shock as well. And then where do they go? Fry the poor creature? I think if it has really got to that stage, both dog and owner would be better going their separate ways: the dog into rescue and the owner into a pit of cobras.

The Dog Won't Sit or Stay

The original puppies in *From Puppy to Perfect* are all pretty much grown up now, and no doubt performing feats of unparalleled perfection all over the country. But a reader complained to me the other day: 'I taught my puppy to sit using your feed bowl technique and he was great to begin with, but now I can't get him to sit or stay.' I asked him if he was still using the feed bowl technique. No, he wasn't. Teaching a pup to sit is really simple and as a result we usually get a bit complacent about it as the pup becomes an adult dog. But, as with all instructions, you must insist that the dog listens to them throughout its life, not just when it was first being trained. If things start going wrong, it's usually because you've stopped bothering to keep on top of them. Frequent revision and practise are needed for all dogs, not just competition dogs.

If you haven't had a chance to teach your dog how to sit, here's what to do. At feed time hold your dog's feed bowl up above his head at the same time as saying 'sit'. The dog will look up at the feed bowl, and as one end of him goes up, the other end inevitably goes down, so the dog ends up sitting at your feet. Wait a second so that he really is sitting up looking at the food bowl, then put the bowl down and let him eat, verbally praising as you do so. If the dog doesn't immediately sit, don't give him the food. Most dogs, even those being taught later in life, get the message fairly quickly. Always remember to give the verbal command 'sit' as you raise the food bowl, so that the dog associates his sitting action with your instruction.

The next stage of this exercise is really simple and yet it is one of the great fundamentals of all dog teaching. I call it the 'Daddy or chips?' moment. Ages ago, a commercial for oven chips asked the question. Some kids were sweet enough to ponder a split second before coming to a conclusion. But in all cases, the answer was the same: Chips! Now, sitting in front of you, as you hold his beloved feed bowl, your dog is facing a 'Daddy or chips?' dilemma, and he is going to be gradually led to the answer: Daddy! A dog that puts the boss before food is a dog that truly respects you, and all the rest follows from there.

As you can see, Fizz learned the sit command from a very early age!

Holding the bowl up, ask the dog to sit as usual. This time make to put the bowl down to one side and slightly behind you, so that you are between the dog and his bowl. The dog will move to the bowl, which you snatch up before he can get it, and repeat the command, sit. Then repeat. The dog will be a little confused and will dither a bit, so put the bowl down completely and praise him. I also use an instruction like 'take it' so the dog knows it's OK to tuck in. Keep playing around with this, always with yourself between the dog and the bowl. Aim to get to the stage where you say sit, the dog sits, and you put the bowl down – but the dog doesn't move until you release him with an instruction and praise. The reason for you being between the dog and the bowl is so that you can grab him if necessary and put him back in his sit position. This simple exercise in respect goes on throughout the dog's life. It's just politeness really. I'm sure you wouldn't let your children start shovelling away before everybody is seated and served, and it's just the same with your dog. And because food is so important to a dog, it sets the tone for all aspects of

As she got older Fizz learnt to obey the command when out and about.

having a polite and pleasant dog who can enjoy a little self-control when required. If there is any question of the dog being a bit snarly or aggressive if you get between it and its food, this is a big danger sign and you should go and read the **Serious Problems** section.

Once your dog understands the 'sit' instruction and responds to it, even with 'chips' as a temptation, teaching him to sit when you are out and about follows quite naturally. In the garden or your training area, ask your dog to sit. At the same time raise your hand up to about eye level with your arm out-stretched and the palm flat, facing slightly forwards, very much like a traffic officer stopping your car. This hand gesture is now basically replacing what you do with a feed bowl: it gets the dog's eyes up, looking attentively at you. The main point is that it can be seen by the dog from quite some distance. This is your visual signal for 'sit'. Do some lessons with this over the next few days. Most dogs cotton on quite quickly, so experiment with the dog being slightly further away from you when you give the commands. Always make sure that the dog's attention is mainly on you when you give the instruction.

Don't repeat the instruction too often, particularly if the dog gets it. Just incorporate it into your daily exercise routine – but do make sure the dog responds promptly every single time you give the 'sit' command. If you want you can add in the whistle as an additional instruction. I prefer to use the whistle rather than 'sit' when I am out and about. It is much more precise, and easier for the dog to hear when it is outdoors. Of course, eventually you may want your dog to sit on command when it is some way away from you – anything up to a couple of hundred metres in some cases.

Hold your whistle in your left hand, ready to pop into your mouth. Put up your hand in the visual sit signal at the same time as commanding 'sit' verbally, and then instantly putting the whistle in your mouth and blowing the single long peeeep. The dog should already have sat before you can get your whistle blown, but that's OK. Repeat this lesson a few times over the next couple of days and then start playing around with the different combinations of the three forms of command. Gradually get to the point where you have your hand raised in the visual signal at the same time as you blow the whistle, without using the verbal command. When

Waiting patiently for a moment before being invited to tuck in is just good manners.

you are practising this combination it helps to have your whistle already in your mouth and to blow it at exactly the same time as you raise your hand. At first you may need to back it up a bit by spitting out your whistle and giving the verbal 'sit' command.

Surprisingly quickly, though, you will find that your dog is responding to just the whistle and your raised hand. When performed at a distance, this is the 'stop' command. It's vital for a lot of different dog competition disciplines and it's also extremely useful for pet dogs. Supposing you, the family and, of course, the dog, are enjoying a country walk. He's off the lead but you suddenly realise that there are sheep running loose or a rabbit pops its ears up. You can stop your dog from chasing after them and getting into trouble just by blowing your stop whistle and the dog will sit and look at you immediately. Now imagine that it's not a field with sheep but a busy road with cars and you can see how it is even more important to have a dog that instantly obeys that 'stop' command. This is especially the case for those living in urban areas where there are so many pressures on space and all sorts of unexpected situations. Teaching your dog this command properly and making sure he is obedient to it will make a huge difference to his life because it means that it will be safe to let him off the lead where appropriate and permitted. Otherwise your urban dog could find itself spending most of its outdoor life tied up to your wrist.

So try this simple exercise. Let the dog get a little further away than usual and then blow the whistle. He will stop, sit and look at you. Walk up to him and give him loads of praise. The reason for you walking to him rather than him coming to you is to make sure he gets into the habit of staying sat still and steady. If your dog isn't very good at staying when he is sat, there are lots of different exercises you can do to help him. Sit your dog up and then try some of the following:

● Walking back – if the dog begins to crawl towards you or lose concentration, then just walk quietly up to him and start again with a fresh 'sit' command.

● Spiralling – to make it easier for the dog to understand that he shouldn't come over to you, you can do your moving away in a spiral, with the distance between you and the pup gradually increasing as you walk in circles around him.

● Re-placing – if the dog comes running towards you, walk up to him and pick him up and take him back to the exact spot where you stopped him.

THE SOCIAL PROBLEMS

For me, this is the most interesting group of problems, and a very popular area of research among animal behaviourists. It is only comparatively recently that we have started to get a true understanding of how socialisation works within animal groups and between animals and humans. The more we learn about the science, the more obvious it becomes that early socialisation experiences have a major effect on brain development, and in turn, behaviour – this goes for humans, too! Failures of socialisation can lead to serious problems such as aggression, which for safety's sake I have addressed briefly at the beginning of the book as well as in the **Serious Problems** section. Socialisation is at the heart of the issues covered here. However, these problems more than any other are subjective. One family may have a big problem with a dog peeing on the duvet, while another may consider it just a normal part of dog owning. It really is a case of 'if it ain't broke, don't fix it'. If you find your dog's behaviour acceptable, there's no need for you to change his socialisation boundaries. But if you do have a problem, then you have to be receptive to the various solutions – some of which may be against your initial instincts.

Dog Doesn't Like Me

A surprisingly large number of dog owners describe a rather abstract problem that can be quite difficult to get your head around. They tend to say something like: 'Oh, I don't know what's wrong. I mean he's reasonably well behaved, he's great with the family and all that, but he just doesn't seem to like me.' The comment quite often comes from the family's main breadwinner. One such dog owner just wasn't hitting it off with his dog at all. He claimed not to be much bothered by this. He'd bought the dog more for the family, and it certainly got on well with the wife and kids, so there you go. But you could see it did bother him. His alpha male ego was piqued when the dog came bounding enthusiastically over to his oldest daughter when she got home from school, but never greeted him at all on his return from work. But it wasn't exactly 'a problem' – and certainly not anything psycho! Then I met the dog owner a few months later, with the dog, both of them grinning from ear to ear. It turned out that during the winter the entire family, with the exception of the husband, had gone down with food poisoning. The job of letting the dog out first thing in the morning and feeding him had fallen to the husband, who'd never done it before. 'It was amazing,' he said. 'I've never seen anyone so happy to see me in my life – humans included! The dog was just turning himself inside out, wagging his tail, rushing around the garden. It made me laugh! Actually, it really cheered me up.'

This man, a massively successful businessman, had never experienced the joyous, unconditional and unthinking love that a dog instinctively lavishes almost randomly on those with whom it connects. A morning

An interesting example of dogs who like their owner in different ways. Ricky is looking at the camera because that is where I am looking and we have a strong bond of working together, so he looks where I look, but Lemon just dotes on me, so is gazing up fondly as usual!

dog is always full of boundless joy and, with his family unwell, the husband had been on the receiving end, for the first time, of the wholehearted 'what an awesome morning, boss' that the rest of his family got every day. Maybe all big businesses should employ a dog or two just to cheer up high flying executives and remind them what it's really all about.

This is why it is so rewarding to solve the problem of 'my dog doesn't like me'. Sometimes, as with the businessman, it sorts itself out on its own. The main reason for this sense of unease between owner and dog is that a bond hasn't developed between them, known to behaviourists as 'attachment failure'. In the case of the businessman, the bond hadn't developed because he had never been the one to feed the dog and let it out first thing in the morning – and this is actually comparatively common in families with a very traditional, conventional structure. The main breadwinner doesn't expect to be closely involved in the dog's care and this means that he ends up missing out on all the nurturing behaviour a dog gives back to its carer.

Generally, the more you put into your relationship with your dog, the more you will get back. Feeding and caring for your dog is the first step, but there is much more to it. When you are out and about together, pay attention to your dog. You may not notice it, but he will certainly be engaged with you. If you concentrate too, you will soon see that your dog notices not just what you say, but also very slight signals from your body language, even where you are looking. Return the compliment. Watch what he is doing and respond to it. Very soon the two of you will be communicating in a really profound way. The more adventures you have together, the greater this bond will become. It is particularly obvious in competition dogs, where the dog and its owner/handler share some great experiences together as they prepare for competitions and then travel all over the country to compete. Shown here is a picture of me and my colleague Jon Bailey, one of the country's top professional spaniel trainers, with three generations of my cockers. The 'oldsters' – Fudge and me – are having a cuddle. Then there is Fudge's son, Ginger, who had just been placed in the national finals, and his daughter, Fizz, who had come along for the ride. It is really obvious to see that Ginger and Fizz, who were being trained by Jon at the time, have eyes only for him, even though on paper they are my dogs!

Hi Bird Photography

Three generations: Fudge, Ginger and Fizz, but Ginger and Fizz only have eyes for Jon Bailey, who is training them at present.

Fan club secretary!

nigeourrphotography.co.uk

When it comes to rescue dogs, establishing a bond can be a big challenge, but so rewarding when you finally succeed. As the human part of the equation with a rescue dog you need to be: utterly reliable, consistent, patient, dependable, tolerant, empathetic, and, above all, trustworthy. The rescue dog will almost certainly have been let down in some way in his past. You will make sure that never happens again, but the dog doesn't know that yet. It's your job to show him that he can trust again. Establish a routine that suits the dog, and really, really stick to it. This is one time where that hot date or family outing does have to take second place. Engage with your rescue dog. Think hard about where he's coming from and why his behaviours have developed. Use your *Dog Day Diary* to help you get an overview. Be prepared that you will have to spend a lot of time with him – and that for much of that time he will just ignore you! Yet you also have to create very clear and secure boundaries for your rescue dog. Your tolerance allows you to accept his behaviours for what they are, but gradually you will be aiming to adapt them to get to the place where you and he are both relaxed and happy. Use all the techniques described throughout this book, but add to them the context of winning his trust and confidence.

When your dog starts off by not liking you very much and ends up being the traditional 'man's best friend', that's a really fulfilling journey. For me, some of these attachment issues fall in the category of problems we'd all like to have! My own breed of dogs are notoriously sociable and well adjusted, and find bonding with pretty much any and every human they come across to be not worthy of comment. Owning them is like being in the gang of the most popular kid in school. Although I like to think they love only me, or at least me best, if I'm honest, my role is probably little more than secretary of their fan club!

My Dog Doesn't Play

Play is such an important part of our lives with our dogs, just as it is in human life generally. We use play as a way of teaching and learning. It is important for relaxation, and playing together aids in attachment and bonding. The more structured version of play – sport – is equally important in development. Behavioural neuroscience is beginning to uncover the process by which both dogs and humans learn through play. It is believed that the relaxed concentration and focus we experience during play and sport induces a 'flow state' in the brain that allows learned material to become embedded, as new neural connections are made within the brain. Research into cognitive deterioration in older people has found it to be significantly reduced where the elderly person is taking part in a 'play' activity such as an exercise class or learning a new sport (even if it's only tiddlywinks!). You can try this for yourself. Find an interesting, but quite challenging, documentary or drama on your iPlayer or radio and have it playing in the background while you are doing something that requires relaxed concentration – perhaps cooking or colouring or decorating. You will be surprised at how much of the information in the documentary stays with you in considerable detail for a long time afterwards. It's a good trick for learning a new language quickly.

It is important for your dog to play and to be able to play. Some breeds and types of dog are by nature not particularly inclined to be playful, while others are complete jokers. Have a think about your dog and other dogs of his breed that you know. Could this be why he doesn't play much? If he's just not that way inclined, you should still try to jolly him along a bit – it's good for him! Sometimes this type of dog responds well to a non-human companion, and bizarrely it doesn't always have to be a dog!

If your dog is normally playful and suddenly stops playing, suspect a health issue. Keep your *Dog Day Diary* to give yourself a more detailed picture of his change in behaviour. Sometimes an obvious reason will become apparent. Perhaps a family member has just gone off to college and the dog was very attached to her. But if nothing comes up, it is worth a trip to the vet for a physical check-up.

The most common cause of a dog not showing play behaviour is inhibition, so you need to find out what is causing the inhibition. With a rescue dog, it is often very obvious that the dog just has no experience of play. He's never had the opportunity to play and he may have been used as a play object, for example by being teased or abused. Along with the general trust work you are doing with the dog, gradually introduce play. He should have his own toys, but be allowed to ignore them or simply own them, as opposed to playing. Never force play on him. Let him come to you. Tactfully watch his body language and react when opportunities to play arise naturally. These might be very simple, like the first time he lets you rub his tum or the first time he brings you something. Other dogs and other animals can be helpful too, in letting the rescue dog observe play at a safe distance. With rescue dogs it's always very important to let them go at their own pace and then celebrate the day they chase their first butterfly!

The other important cause of play inhibition in your dog is sometimes difficult for the owner to accept. If the household and family environment in which the dog lives is not conducive to play, the dog will not feel secure to play. His lack of opportunity to play may not appear to cause difficulties initially, but gradually a number of problems will appear. The dog won't be so trainable. He will be very easily stressed and will probably develop chronic stress-relief behaviours. He may even become timid/aggressive or develop health issues. This is really the flip side of the family that has no boundaries for the dog. In this instance there are likely to be too many rules and boundaries. The long term effect is similar in both cases. The issue often arises in households that have one very dominant family member who lays down the law for everybody – including the dog. Often people are very house proud and very particular about the garden and the lawns and flowerbeds. This leaves the dog with no space to play, and an atmosphere that is not conducive to play.

If you recognise this situation, it might be that the whole family would benefit from a little more play. Don't panic – this doesn't mean chaos or conflict. It can be done in a structured way that everybody will be comfortable with. The dog and one or more family members can join a dog training or dog activity club. Have a look at The Kennel

Club website (details at the back of the book) and find all the many different clubs locally. This gives the chance for the dog to get out and socialise and play outside the home environment at least once a week, and it's probably no bad thing that a family member has to go along with it. At home, if the garden really is too precious for play, arrange for the dog and a family member to visit a neighbour or friend to borrow their garden to play in or go to a local park. And in the house, set aside a small area that can be 'dog-land'. It can have its own special sign saying 'Dog's Place' or whatever, so that everybody knows why it might be a bit less tidy than elsewhere. In this way, giving the dog opportunities to play and expand his horizons can often allow the whole household to start looking outward, and maybe give relaxation all round!

Case History: Daphne, a Gold Medal Dog

Caroline and her cocker-poo, Daphne, have been working their way through the various Kennel Club obedience awards, which they are both enjoying, and

recently passed the Gold Medal, although Caroline reports: 'Our most unreliable task is when she has to stay while I go out the room for thirty seconds. She lays down with her head stretching up like a meerkat worrying where I'm off to!'

Caroline knows that her gorgeous cocker-poo is the kind of highly intelligent dog that benefits from structured play, as well as creating a bond between them.

Caroline's Gold Medallist cocker-poo, Daphne.

Learning Difficulties

Canine intelligence is every bit as varied as human intelligence. Over the years I have had some dogs who would definitely have been brain surgeons if only they'd had opposable thumbs. I think Tippy was probably more intelligent than me, and I've got two masters degrees. Equally, dear old Dutch was lovely, and handsome and perfect in every way except one – he was undeniably dim. And as for Toffee! Well at least four leading professional dog trainers, scarred to this day by the experience of 'helping out' with Toffee, will tell you that he had learning difficulties.

Genuine learning difficulties do indeed arise in dogs. Due to the way a bitch gives birth, there can sometimes be a problem where a larger than usual pup gets stuck in the birth canal and the pup behind in the queue to come out can be deprived of oxygen. Lack of oxygen to the brain at this crucial stage is associated with learning difficulties that sometimes only become apparent as the pup begins to grow up. There are also other physiological reasons, and even dietary problems may be a contributory factor.

This is quite rare and it can be very difficult to diagnose whether a dog is naughty or genuinely experiences difficulty learning and remembering its lessons. There are some simple canine IQ tests at the beginning of the book that will help, but even these are sometimes deceptive. I think the real telltale sign is when everything goes brilliantly with the dog one day and then it's right back to square one again the next day. One of my friends, suffering under the curse of Toffee, said exasperatedly: 'He's more like a goldfish than a dog. He learns the lesson perfectly, but by the time he's done a circuit of the goldfish bowl, it's like it never happened!'

Poor concentration and poor memory are the two big indicators that your unfortunate dog may not be quite all there upstairs. Keep your *Dog Day Diary* and look out especially for signs of on-off behaviour in your dog. You can also try a couple of specific tests. Put your dog's favourite toy in a semi-accessible hiding place in the garden. With any luck he will want to go and get it. Let him. Just before bedtime, let him see you put his favourite toy back in exactly that same spot, but don't allow him to get it this time. Instead put him to bed as usual. In the morning, let him out and watch what he does. A reasonably intelligent dog will have a quick wee and then shoot straight over to where his toy was left the previous night and pick it up. Retrieving breeds will remember where something is hidden for weeks afterwards. This is irritating if you put the manky thing in the skip because you wanted to throw it away and the dog keeps bringing it back into the house for weeks. But at least it shows they are intelligent and have a good memory. The learning difficulty dog is likely to have a hard time finding his toy; he may even completely forget to go and look for it.

Another test is to teach your dog to find a food treat in your pocket. Put the treat in your pocket and indicate to the dog that it is there by patting your pocket. Every dog knows the treat is there, not because you patted your pocket, but because he can smell it. Spend the day teaching your dog to come and get his treat when you pat your pocket, and give him the treat every time. Don't play the game again for a couple of days. Then test your dog by patting your empty pocket and inviting him to come for the treat. An intelligent dog will come for the treat because he has made the association between you patting your pocket and the prospect of a treat. Even though today, he can't actually smell the treat, the association will be enough for him to come and check you out at least on the off chance. But a challenged dog won't smell a treat, and therefore he won't come. He has failed to make the association between pocket patting and the possibility of a treat. The necessary neural connections in his brain haven't been created in the way that would occur with a normal dog.

This is why a learning difficulty dog is so hard to train, and why the 'goldfish syndrome' is such a problem. A huge amount of dog training is based on memory and association. We reinforce these associations with any number of different rewards, which in turn serve to cement the new neural connections we are creating. Without this process working with a challenged dog can be immensely frustrating, nor is it curable. The best thing is to gain an awareness of your dog's learning difficulties, accept them and adapt to them. While you are still not sure if your dog's behaviour is due to learning issues, try to get opinions from experienced people. Join a local dog training class and see how your dog gets on compared with his peer group. You may well discover that everything is fine, and that the two of you were just on the wrong track. But it may become obvious that your dog doesn't have the same capacities as other dogs in the class.

At least you know! It took us all ages to accept that Toffee was just a nitwit rather than naughty. Once we had finally come to terms with our Toffee 'failure' we found an excellent home for him living in the middle of some moorland with an owner who adored him and had no need or desire for a well-trained dog. Eventually (and unexpectedly) Toffee became a father, and all his offspring were normal, bright, trainable dogs. So it all ended happily ever after. And it can with your dog, too. Be aware of his issues and don't try to demand too much from him. If you are in public spaces, keep him on a flexi-lead, as he could well forget to come back when called. This won't really be deliberate, as it is with most dogs who don't come. It could be just that he is easily distracted, has poor concentration and has genuinely not made the link between you calling and his returning. Be prepared that you are going to have to do most of his thinking for him. So always try to be alert, and aware about where and when there are risks of things going a bit pear-shaped. As long as you learn to live with your challenged dog's limitations, he can make a great family pet, even though chaos may always be just around the corner!

Obsessive Behaviour

The obsessive compulsive group of behaviours used to be seen frequently in zoo-kept animals, intensively farmed animals and often in animals used for performing. Fortunately there is now a much stronger awareness, at least in Western developed countries, of the extreme mental discomfort these behaviours indicate in the animals exhibiting them. Even today though we can probably all think of recent examples: the intensively farmed hen that has compulsively pecked out all its own feathers, the zoo tiger whose cage pacing has actually worn a groove in the ground in front of the bars. I am no vegetarian, but as far as possible I eat only wild-reared animal products. I have seen dairy cows that have chewed off their own tails or are hopping lame. Pigs in close confinement may even start to chew each other. All these obsessive compulsive behaviours develop from the stress of being kept not only in unnatural confinement, but also in conditions where natural activities such as grass chewing, lying down, scratching, wandering and mutual grooming with another animal are impossible. I imagine this is making you as angry to read as it is me to write, so let's move on to how we can diagnose and cure these problems if we come across them with our dogs.

Unfortunately, obsessive compulsive behaviour does occasionally occur with dogs and, even more regrettably, it has similar causes. When an animal is in a stressful situation it will often undertake what is called a 'displacement activity'. This is an activity that gives it a moment of distraction from the stressful event, literally 'displacing' it and thus allowing the animal to cope better with whatever is going on. The effect can be quite comical. I'm sure we've all seen online videos of animals in the middle of really kicking off when one of them suddenly breaks off and starts licking its bits or eating a banana! And actually, in human life, who of us has not taken a step back from a blazing row by deciding the kettle needs to be put on or there is a very pressing text to be attended to, or indeed eating a banana (any other activities are none of my business!).

These displacement activities are useful in giving relief and often take the heat right out of a situation, allowing the source of stress to subside. Problems arise when there is no opportunity to perform the displacement activity or when the stress is so continuous that the dog performs it repeatedly, eventually becoming addicted to it. So a dog that is pretty stressed by something in its environment might start licking its backside or chewing its paws. If the environment remains extremely stressful it will start to lick or chew itself compulsively, to the point where parts of its body may become bald or its paw may get infected.

Bald spots and repeated paw infections are among the most common symptoms. Others include ritualised actions similar to those of humans with obsessive compulsive disorder. Where a human checks the iron is switched off a dozen times, a dog may pick up its toy and put it in its bed repeatedly. Or it may urinate time and again, even though each is the merest dribble. If you are beginning to suspect that your dog is becoming obsessive, get the *Dog Day Diary* out. How often is he doing this behaviour? Is it leading to health problems including infections, bald spots or exhaustion? Can you identify triggers for his behaviour? Most of all you need to think very carefully and honestly about his day-to-day living environment. Is he getting free play and running? Is he getting plenty of outdoor activity? Does he have sufficient stimulation? And most of all, what is causing him to feel stressed?

Really only you can answer those questions. Only you are on site every day to know the ins and outs of your dog's life. Perhaps you live in a busy block of flats in the middle of town? Noisy neighbours playing drum'n'bass music at all hours is going to be every bit as stressful for your dog as it is for you. And there may be many other, far more subtle, stressors. Are you frequently kept late at work so that your dog is left at home for an additional two or three hours waiting for the loo and dinner? Is your dog bullied by other animals or even humans? Does your dog have no space of his own? Do you have challenging behaviours yourself, such as substance abuse? If your dog keeps seeing you suddenly change personality he will get very stressed.

The good thing is that you have bought and are reading this

book, so you have already made a huge commitment to help your dog. Now you have a wonderful opportunity to follow up on that by being open and accepting in acknowledging the truth of your dog's situation. If that reality has a bearing on your own situation or lifestyle, congratulate yourself on having the courage to admit that and realise that it could be the beginning of a rewarding journey that you and your dog make together.

Much of the time the source of your dog's compulsive activity will be easy to spot and simple to solve. It could just be as obvious as next door's dog regularly getting the chance to access your dog's territory and bully it. As soon as you have a good idea of what is going on, the first thing to do is change the situation. Even quite small changes, such as moving the dog's bed, may be enough. Changing and adapting routines and letting your dog call the tune is an important part of the cure.

This may not always be enough. If your dog has developed health problems as a result of his compulsion then it's time to visit the vet, who will be able to give you lots of specific advice. One technique that can be helpful is to replace a harmful compulsion with some less unhealthy activity. In other words, substitute a bad habit with a good habit. This needs to be handled carefully in case the new habit eventually becomes equally negative. In the case of a dog that is constantly licking and chewing its paws, it is instinctive to have the idea of giving it a bone to chew instead. But this is a bit like a hardened smoker switching to an e-cigarette; the addiction to nicotine remains the same. Instead, try to change the environment and the circumstances leading up to the behaviour. A human smoker often feels his or her compulsion to smoke much more strongly at certain times – perhaps with a drink, after a meal or before an important meeting. So try to remove the triggers or introduce new distractions to prevent the triggers acting. If you see your dog start to lick his paws, take him out for a walk. If he's compulsively picking up his toy, give him a big cuddle or take him for a play date with a dog he likes. Learning new activities can make a huge difference to a compulsive dog. CaniX is a leisure activity where dogs and their owners go cross-country running together and there are lots of other low stress, but structured, sports you can do with your dog. Learning a new skill readjusts the neural pathways in his brain as well as getting him out of the environment that has been stressing him. A quick internet trawl will give you mounds of information about what you and your dog can get up to, and there is a description of the main activities in *From Puppy to Perfect*. Don't say you haven't time, because you do: You have time to change your dog's life, and quite possibly your own.

Chewing/Barking

Although dog owners complain a great deal to me about their dogs that constantly bark or chew inappropriately, they all seem to share a sense of fatalism about it that makes me wonder why they complain in the first place. When I worked in the tough world of Fleet Street tabloid newspapers the going could, undeniably, get rough. Occasionally things might get so apparently unbearable for a sheltered young woman in her twenties that she would hang around outside the editor's office in the hope of getting a chance of a whinge. Believe me, you never did that more than once. The editor's (forcible, and perhaps with more ****s than I can reproduce here) would always be along the lines of: 'Put up or shut up. If you don't like it, fix it. If you can't fix it, **** off.'

I suppose I have been hardened because I always want to say to dog owners about their chewing or barking dogs: 'If you don't like it, fix it. If you can't be bothered to fix it, then stop moaning!' You know, if Pepper has chewed your favourite Mulberry handbag to bits, then who is to blame? A dog, which is by nature designed to chew? Or the idiot who left him alone with an expensive handbag for that length of time.

However, I am not a tabloid newspaper editor, so I will not say these things. I will merely comment that a dog has a health and mental need to chew. Chewing is good for its teeth and gums and also provides mental relaxation. So your dog should always have access to purpose-designed chews. I prefer veterinary-approved dental chews, but any of the wide range available will do the job. Special dog bones and similar organic chews based on hide, etc, are also fine. Country-dwelling dogs find all kinds of ghastly things to chew and almost never come to any harm, even if what they are chewing looks to you more horrid than a newspaper editor.

When it comes to your dog chewing the wrong thing, there are a number of reasons, all equally solvable. Has he got the right thing available to chew? Is the wrong thing within temptingly easy reach to chew? Is he being left alone for long periods with no stimulation? If you leave your young child alone to play with crayons and no colouring book, you won't be surprised when he crayons on the walls. Similarly, if you leave the dog alone in the living room for hours with nothing to chew, don't be surprised when he chews the furniture. Make sure your dog has a stimulating environment and that he's not left alone with free run of the house for long periods of time. If you have to leave the dog alone, make sure he has his own dog pen to be in and give him plenty of his toys to chew and scrag.

Although barking really comes from the same place as unwanted chewing, it is a more difficult problem to deal with, and can tip over into obsessive compulsive behaviour. Remember, too, that barking is not just an issue for you, but can be a massive stress for your neighbours, who have to suffer something they can do nothing about. Constantly yapping, barking and whining is also a symptom of other problems, so needs thinking about.

Don't be tempted to take easy, forced solutions to barking. An internet browse will come up with all sorts of mechanical remedies for barking, which merely mask or muzzle the problem, as opposed to solving it. As I have mentioned, Tippy was an exceptionally intelligent dog. Like me, she had a low boredom threshold and almost no tolerance of idiots. This found her out from time to time in her competition work. On one occasion, during a national final, she was required to sit and watch and wait while another dog performed its work. Tippy and I agreed on one thing: the other dog was useless. Tippy emoted to me that her patience had run out and that she would shortly be taking over from the useless canine. In due course she did so and that was the end of the competition for us. In retirement, Tippy found kennel life to be equally lacking in action, particularly as, once again, she found herself surrounded by dim dogs who didn't know their Euclid from their elbow. So, out of boredom, she got a bit yappy. I bought an ingenious collar that was triggered to deliver a small, harmless burst of citronella spray each time her voice box moved to bark. It worked, in a way. Tippy stopped barking loudly, but she adored the citronella shot so she learned how to work the collar and get a regular fix. The real solution (which I expect Tippy had engineered all along) was for Tippy to come indoors into my study and be a writer's dog. In due course her daughter, Fudge (illustrated), did the same.

Fudge's retirement role as a writer's dog.

Finding out why your dog is barking or yapping will often give you the immediate solution. In neighbourhoods with a lot of dogs, particularly ones who live outside during the day, the barking is usually triggered by one dog at a time and then the others join in. Living in a rural village with plenty of farm dogs in the area can be a nightmare, as they all set each other off, right through the night. This is a case for being a bit community minded and getting all the different dog owners together for a chat, which is not always easy. In a village I lived in, there was a farmyard right in the heart of the village, near the pub. At chucking out time there were always kids hanging round near the farmyard, setting off the farm's guard dog at 2 a.m.. We got it sorted in the end, but on this occasion we did have to involve the community police officer.

Don't let things get that far with your dog. If his barking has a specific trigger, such as people walking past on the road, then you need to change the position of his dog-place. Has his barking become compulsive? In other words, is he barking when there is no apparent trigger? Check out the obsessive compulsive section where you will find help in easing him out of this habitual behaviour. Or is he barking out of aggression? Does his barking easily tip over into snarling and growling? Have a look at the **Serious Problems** section for help on this. One of the most underestimated causes of constant barking is lack of stimulation in the dog's environment. I have often wondered if this kind of barking is simply a protective mechanism for the dog to try to get attention or perhaps connect with another dog that might be within earshot, to ease its loneliness. If your dog is a sole dog, it is well worth thinking about getting another to give him someone to interact with, rather than simply howling at the wall. I have found that having two dogs is no more and occasionally actually less trouble than one dog, and I think it is a much more positive solution for your lonely dog than just leaving the telly switched on.

Remember, too, that vocalisation is normal for a dog and it is part of his repertoire of self-expression. Dogs that live together in a group will often sing together, usually after their evening meal. It's a bonding activity that doesn't last for long that can be quite fun to listen to on a summer's evening, though it's not particularly melodious. Dogs will also bark out of overexcitement, usually when they are heading off for playtime, and, again, that's nothing to worry about. Other barks are used to warn off other dogs, to warn you of danger or if the dog is suddenly in pain. If your dog gets caught up in barbed wired or something similar, he'll usually bark for help, so always investigate an unexpected bark.

Won't House-Train

Second to pulling on the lead, house-training issues are among the most frequent problems people bring me. But I'm also surprised by how much failed house-training some dog owners will tolerate. Do you remember *The Osbournes* reality TV show? It starred of course, Ozzy Osbourne and his charmingly eccentric family, but the show was regularly stolen by the household's various dogs and their lavatory habits. How can you be a multi-millionaire and live basically in a heap of s***, we viewers asked ourselves, tuning in again and again to see what fresh steaming piles would be discovered and where! But for Ozzy, really it wasn't that much of a problem, certainly not compared with everything else that was always kicking off.

And here we normal folk do actually have something in common with superstar rock and rollers. Like the Osbournes, the house-training of our dogs comes down to how much of a priority it is for us. If you lead a chaotic lifestyle and really can't be that bothered about house-training your dog and giving him regular toilet opportunities, then you are going to have to accept that accidents will happen. Perhaps this is what Elvis Costello was singing about in his 1979 hit *Accidents Will Happen*? Perhaps all rock stars have incontinent dogs? My point is that if you won't get up at 7 a.m. to let the dog out for a wee, then don't come complaining to me when you have to walk through a puddle on the kitchen floor to get to the kettle!

Of course, we all want full and happy lives, which will inevitably be extremely full and very happy from time to time, and there is absolutely no need to sacrifice ourselves 24/7 to our dogs' lavatory requirements. However, the most important element in keeping your dog regular is to keep his routine regular. A dog that is fed at the same time each day and toileted and exercised and given down times at the same time each day will also go to the loo at the same time each day. As long as there is someone there to give the dog access to wherever his loo spot may be then there is no problem with house-training.

Even from very earliest puppyhood that is basically all there is to house-training. Since this book is about adult dogs, if you are house-training a puppy, I recommend you check out the section in *From Puppy to Perfect*, which covers initial house-training in detail, including provision for city dogs who may be using an indoor toilet. Read on now if your adult dog is having problems.

First of all, the *Dog Day Diary* is important to give you an idea of why the dog is not house-trained. Note down the dog's daily routine, and yours. Usually this is the root cause of the problem. It will probably become obvious that either your routines are not in sync or you have very little routine at all. The obvious solution is to create a routine that works for you both – but that may be easier said than done! If your dog is fed on proprietary dog food twice a day, with few titbits, it is likely he will defecate twice a day. If you feed him morning and evening, again those are the most likely times of day for him to need a dump. So you immediately have control over that. Work out a time or times of day that you can reliably be available to feed your dog and take him outdoors for ten or fifteen minutes. If there really is no possibility of you being available that regularly then recruit family members and friends to help you. If that isn't possible either it may be time for a little introspection. How come you are unable to give your dog even this very minor fixed reference point in his life? Although my dogs are important to me both personally and professionally, I don't put them first in my private life. Yet no matter how intensely or unexpectedly I may find myself partying, I can always slip away for long enough to let the dogs go to the loo or I can send an emergency text to a mate. The dogs look at me very strangely as I stagger out in the morning, holding my head carefully in a stable position, but they get their comfort break and breakfast all the same.

Helping your dog to control his bladder is more difficult as the dog will obviously need to wee more often and at less predictable intervals. And, of course, in common with so many mammals including humans, dogs are able to wee at will, so you may also face the issue of hidden agendas. First of all, let's assume that the dog is weeing in the wrong place because either he doesn't know it's the wrong place or he can't get to the right place.

Giving him the opportunity to get to the right place is a good start. Let him have a quick loo run first thing in the morning; before and after playtime; before and after meeting people (whether strangers or family); before and after down times; before his bedtime; and last thing at night before you go to bed (or out clubbing, you don't have to be a saint to have a house-trained dog!). This may sound like a massive commitment, but you don't have to do it at this level for very long. Nor do you need to spend more than a couple of minutes each time. Most dogs have a wee as the first thing they do when going outside, so your mission will be accomplished swiftly. Do remember though, that it is very important not to rush the dog straight back into the house the moment he has been to the loo. Dogs love being outside with you, even if it's only just for a quick sniff around the lawn. By dragging him straight back inside the second he's weed, you're giving him the message that going to the loo means the end of playtime. So you could end up with a dog that holds on and crosses his legs just to keep on playing! I have fallen into this mistake when house-training puppies, and the long, freezing wait in dressing gown and slippers at ten o'clock on a winter's evening, while puppy plays around cutely without emptying his bladder is one of the less rewarding aspects of dog ownership. So go on playing with your dog for a minute or two after he's been. Give him some verbal praise. Some people like to use a verbal cue such as 'get busy' while the dog is going to the loo, although personally I haven't found this to be particularly effective. Don't give your dog a food reward as you could set up an association in your dog's mind between weeing and begging for a food treat. Then you will end up still with a puddle on the kitchen floor, with the dog sitting alongside it expecting his piece of sausage!

As you follow this routine pretty strictly for a couple of weeks you will soon find that accidents dry up (literally!) as the dog gets into the habit of going outside, but not indoors.

Soon your dog will become confident enough to know that he will get an opportunity to empty his bladder, and you will find that he does start holding on until that moment arrives. This is when you will be able to be less rigorous with some of the toilet breaks. Don't let your dog down by sliding back into old habits and leaving him for long periods without the opportunity to empty his bladder. He's showing trust in you by waiting for you to take him to the loo and if he loses that trust then you'll soon be back to random weeing. If he's no confidence that you will ever turn up and let him out why should he wait at all?

Another question to ask yourself is whether your dog actually knows he's weeing in the wrong place? A reader was complaining to me that his young dog was constantly getting upstairs and weeing on the bed. This presupposes that you don't want the dog upstairs. If you do want the dog upstairs you have to get used to the fact that the occasional accident on the bed is almost inevitable. But if the dog is getting into the bedroom when he's not meant to then the wee on the bed is almost certainly out of anxiety because the dog has realised that he's got into this place where he's not really meant to be. With a very dominant dog it can also be a bit of a power play: 'Look, I own this bed now!' In either case, the answer is fairly straightforward. Had you considered shutting the bedroom door? Or putting a gate at the bottom of the stairs? Or putting the dog in his pen when you can't supervise his play? I can imagine any number of young dogs who, if they could, would write to ask me: 'I'm so worried about my human, she keeps leaving the bedroom door open and I've no idea whether I'm meant to be in there or not?'

The whole question of the dog in the bedroom, whether weeing or not, is one we've discussed often in this book. If you don't have a problem and it isn't a problem, that's absolutely fine. Where the dog is allowed to be is an individual choice for each family. But that is an issue in itself – particularly if the dog does then have an accident. When it comes to 'un-house-trainable' dogs, there can be some difficult underlying tensions that are much more human than canine. Remember *The Osbournes*? One of the things that made it such compulsive viewing was the various family dynamics being played out – many of which we might have recognised ourselves! And in some families, when war is imminent, the weapon of choice is the dog and the ammunition is his wee. If one member of the family wants to wind up another member then, gosh, the dog just happens to have got into that person's bedroom and, oh dear, he's had an accident on the *Frozen* duvet cover.

As the dog's responsible person, I think it's important for you to be aware of these possibilities and to come out of denial if the dog is indeed being used in family politics. It is a form of passive aggression to fight out issues through surrogates. How about leaving the dog out of it and confronting the human behaviours? Your dog will certainly thank you. Many dogs find house-training difficult because the fraught human atmosphere in the house is causing them a lot of tension and stress, resulting in panic wees. And if the dog has become very insecure as a result of all this it could also be using wee in an effort to mark out some territory and claim a place where it can feel safe from all the worrying vibes going on around it. This is one of those occasions where our dogs are often trying to tell us something, and if we can manage to hear and engage everybody is better off as a result.

THE HEALTH-RELATED PROBLEMS

It is easy to be cross and judgemental with dog owners who bring me these health-related problems, because basically it is a simple matter of poor animal management on the part of the dog's Responsible Person. But I am originally from an urban environment and my first childhood experience of animals was Harry the Hamster – who turned out to be Harriet, which shows you how much we knew about animal health! Things that seem blindingly obvious to those brought up around animals can be baffling to people from a different background. So don't beat yourself up about possibly having caused your dog some discomfort through not spotting a health-related problem – but now you know, do get on with sorting it out immediately!

Weight Loss/Weight Gain

Most cases of weight loss or gain are not emergencies. It's something quite gradual that takes a while to notice. Usually you will discover that dear old Dasher's increasing girth is down to a very human problem of eating more and dashing less as he goes into retirement. Or young Scooby's inability to gain weight is due to a hefty dose of worms!

Even quite sudden weight loss isn't always serious, but if your dog's weight change is really acute and dramatic then you will need to go straight to the vet. Sudden weight loss accompanied by lack of co-ordination (wobbliness) can be caused by severe dehydration, which your vet will address. Sudden abdominal distension (swelling) could be due to an internal bleed. So if things are happening quickly and you are in any doubt at all, go straight to your vet. Do also remember that if your dog has recently had any sort of trauma (e.g. a car accident or been kicked), symptoms of internal damage can take a while to appear.

You also need to visit your vet as soon as possible if the dog's weight change is accompanied by a range of other symptoms that may be less dramatic, but definitely obvious. Check out these additional signs:

When to Act

● If your dog continues to lose or gain weight quite noticeably

● If weight change continues, despite the dog eating precisely the same amount of food. Be sure about this. Make absolutely certain that no one has been feeding the dog extra. Check that no other dog or animal is stealing the dog's food. Have you changed dog food brand? Or feeding regime? Is the dog able to steal food from sources you don't know about?

- If your dog's personality changes

- If your dog is coughing or retching

- If your dog appears abnormally bloated, its abdomen seems very swollen or it seems to have developed lumps or bumps elsewhere

- If the dog's stools are loose, full of worms or show signs of blood

- If the dog is drinking much more water than usual

- If the dog is hardly ever weeing or only in dribbles

- If the dog is not producing stools

- If the dog doesn't seem able to chew or swallow properly

- If the dog is vomiting constantly

- If the dog ever coughs or vomits blood-stained material

When to Watch

If the change in your dog's weight is not particularly noticeable or has happened over a period of time and is not accompanied by other symptoms then you need to do some careful observation before you go into action. First of all, use an adapted version of your *Dog Day Diary* to monitor your dog's weight. You will need to record the dog's weight for about four to six weeks to see whether it is continuing to change, is remaining the same or is going back towards normal. If your dog is a holdable size you can use the scales at home. Weigh yourself and record the weight (hem, hem, this isn't about your weight, this is about the dog's weight!). Then weigh yourself while carrying the dog. Subtract one from the other and you have the dog's weight. If the dog is too big to lift then you can use the animal weighing scale at your vet's surgery. Vets are happy to get involved in healthy animal weight management and often hold doggy diet classes.

If the dog's weight returns to normal then you can stop worrying. Like humans, dogs' weights fluctuate harmlessly for all sorts of reasons. Competition dogs in hard work often lose weight by the end of the competition season. Entire male dogs sometimes lose weight when a particularly special smelling female causes them to think about only one thing, and it's not food! Sometimes a dog may gain weight temporarily from a change in circumstances in the home – they might not be getting as much exercise as normal – then, when things go back to normal, so does the dog's weight.

If the dog's changed weight remains the same, again, it's not something to worry too much about. Just keep monitoring it from time to time. Some dogs just do gain or lose a bit of weight as they get older. It can be that they get a little bit fatter or lose muscle tone because their lifestyle is gradually winding down. Some females gain a bit of weight after being spayed due to a change in their hormones, but usually it settles down and your vet will advise on a special diet at the time of the operation. Fluctuations in hormones throughout a dog's life can cause minor but harmless weight changes. And, of course, bear in mind that a young dog may just have had a normal growth spurt.

Your *Dog Day Diary* will usually give you the answers to your dog's gradual change in weight. Most frequently it is discovered that someone else has been feeding the dog extra or he has been getting more titbits than usual or less exercise. So the answer is obvious! Sometimes when a dog slims down a bit the reason is because whoever was feeding the dog extra has stopped doing so. Maybe Gran has returned home after a long visit? Or the next door neighbour has moved house? Or you have started jogging and the dog is joining in? With the help of the *Dog Day Diary*, niggling problems become just a matter of common sense. But if you're still not confident about your dog's weight most vets offer dog weight management classes, often free of charge.

Appetite Loss

This issue is closely linked to the weight problems discussed above, but it is worth thinking about on its own because it can also be a problem on its own rather than a symptom of something more complex. Their dogs' lack of appetite is something dog owners frequently report as a worry. Luckily, the majority of appetite loss problems are neither serious nor difficult to solve.

The main cause of appetite loss that I come across is so simple, and it really is just a matter of common sense. The dog's not eating because the dog's not hungry! Doh! I learned this lesson at the age of eleven when looking after my first pony. Off Shandy and I went to Pony Club Camp, full of excitement and loaded up with pony cubes, bran, hay, grooming brushes, hoof oil, tack, jodhpurs and all sorts of specialist kit that fascinated and horrified my parents in equal parts (I now suspect the cost was the main cause of the horror). I fed Shandy religiously as I'd been instructed, with various amounts of cubes, bran and hay and, of course, a little bit extra because she was such a very special pony. By about the second day I was devastated to discover that she wasn't eating and appeared to have lost all appetite! I rushed to Mr Dixon, who was running the horse management side of things, and he came along to inspect my plump little pony. 'Nah then, Janet,' he said, calmly. 'No need to worry, lass, you've just been overfeeding it.' He gave me a new feed list, which I followed carefully, and very shortly afterwards everything was fine. 'Well done, Janet,' said Mr Dixon. If only there were always a Mr Dixon around to make life so simple!

So be a Mr Dixon to your dog. Your dog is almost certainly

not hungry because his tummy is already full! Now you have to ask yourself what it is exactly that may be filling up your dog's stomach. And this is an important question because it's almost certainly not stuff that you actually want to be in your dog's stomach.

The leading culprit here is worms, especially with younger dogs. Once a dog has a heavy worm burden these bloat the stomach and put him off his food. You may see worms in his stools and with tapeworm you can sometimes see little wormlet sections around the dog's anus, looking like grains of rice. Even if you have wormed your dog the wormer may not have been effective, so always suspect worms! Go to your vet and get a veterinary worming programme in place. Use the stickers provided to make sure you keep to the schedule.

Less yuckily, your dog's tum may, of course, already be full of food that someone else has given it without telling you or that it has stolen. The kind of close observation discussed earlier in the book will help you do some detective work on this. Have a look at your *Dog Day Diary*. Does the dog regularly go missing briefly on the day the bin bags go out? It could be stealing next door's leftover pizza or curry once a week. Or, if you're honest, is it getting pizza and curry on a regular basis? In other words, do you frequently give it titbits from the human meals?

There are so many reasons why it is bad for your dog to get a lot of human titbits. In this section we'll stay with those related purely to his health. Both dogs and humans are technically omnivores – that is, we can eat basically anything, sometimes every single edible thing we can lay paws or hands on! But just because we can, doesn't mean that we should eat everything. Just as many human beings have food allergies and intolerances to certain substances, so do dogs. The dangers of chocolate are well known and many dogs are intolerant of gluten, lactose and food colourings, and additives. Good quality prepared dog foods are medically tested, but the stuff you're slipping him under the dining table on pizza night is not. I've come across dog owners spending a fortune on hypo-allergenic dog food yet then giving the dog cupcakes and Chinese takeaway as treats! So if your dog is off the food he's meant to be eating, do be honest with yourself about what else he might be eating.

Occasionally a dog may eat something truly terrible, like a plastic carrier bag, a fish hook or an entire tea towel, without your knowing. If this has happened, you will usually be able to see other signs of distress such as retching or even biting at the stomach. Get to the vet quickly, and don't feel silly if it turns out to be OK (equally don't be embarrassed by what the vet may remove from your dog's stomach!).

A change in routine or stressful events can also put your dog off his food for a while. My dogs often get very excited during the competition season and it can be hard to get them to concentrate on finishing up their meal. Normally they are fed twice a day, morning and early evening, but if they are not eating up well I may change that to four small 'snacks' through the day. Generally though, it's good for dogs to have very regular mealtimes. As mentioned, unlike humans, sex is something that can put an un-neutered male dog off his food! So if there is an 'interesting' female dog in the area be aware of this. And make sure that your male dog doesn't go off and do something about it (her!).

Generally, once you have checked out the worm issue and made sure there are no other accompanying symptoms, loss of appetite for a short time is not something to worry about. If it does go on and other symptoms start showing up then it's time to go to the vet.

Bowel Irregularity/Vomiting

So many dog health issues are centred on its digestive tract, but really, as owners we just have to human up and deal with it. A wife of a keen dog owner was complaining to me about having to poop-scoop and told me that she couldn't possibly go anywhere near a dog's excrement. This lady had four young children and I'm afraid the vision of her trying to change one of her baby's nappies without going anywhere near it made me laugh out loud. Whether you have dogs or not, life is sometimes bad, but we just have to get on with it.

This is very much the case when it comes to your dog having bowel irregularities or vomiting. Most of the time these are nothing to worry about, apart from the cleaning up issue. Bramble was a pup from the first litter I ever bred. When he was a youngster of about six months old he came rushing into the kitchen from playing in the garden. Collapsing in a dramatic heap at my feet, he gazed up at me imploringly, with his soft, brown eyes, emoting as clearly as a dog can do: 'Goodbye, boss, I'm dying now, and so young ...' As I reached for the phone to call the vet, Bramble projectile vomited and evacuated from both ends at once, like some sort of jet-powered vehicle. He then got up, shook himself off and, wagging his tail, trotted back out into the garden, leaving me with a clean up job that makes me shudder to this day. Frequently though, a dog will save you the problem of cleaning up when it has vomited by eating it up itself! I'm not deliberately trying to gross you out, but just explaining that dogs consider vomiting to be, on the whole, just one of those things.

It is the same with loose bowel movements. I have to confess that my dogs' favourite treat on a frosty morning is frozen cow pats, christened 'Poopsicles' after the American name for ice lolly, which is popsicle. No matter how well trained, I can't get them to 'leave' every single frozen cow pat – but surprisingly these do not seem to upset their stomachs in any way!

So the occasional bout of diarrhoea or chundering shouldn't be too serious. Generally it's just a matter of keeping the dog on something very plain such as chicken and rice for a day or two. Make sure the dog always has plenty of water, and keep an eye out to check he's drinking plenty. Dehydration is a danger if a dog has very loose bowels or is being sick.

If the situation is prolonged – chronic – then close observation is necessary. Is the dog managing to regularly get hold of and eat something that could be causing its problems? Does it have worms? These are the normal things you are always asking yourself, as you can see from the problems outlined above. Or the dog may have an intolerance of the particular brand of dog food you are giving it or, of course, those titbits.

Sometimes the cause may be a mental stress that you haven't considered. Is your lifestyle very erratic? Do you tend to feed the dog at all sorts of odd moments, whenever you get round to it? Are there a lot of comings and goings at the house? Does the dog have a safe, secure place where he can eat his meal undisturbed? Just like humans, stressful and random lives can lead to all sorts of digestive problems.

There may also be an underlying physical health issue, perhaps even a tumour, which could be causing the problem. So if you've carefully checked through all your observations and the dog still isn't getting better after a few days – and may be beginning to show other symptoms as well – then it's off to the vet.

Car Sickness

Some of the least serious problems we come across with our dogs can be the hardest to solve and very inconvenient to live with. Car sickness in a dog is one of those problems. Certain breeds, including Labrador retrievers, seem especially prone to it. Terriers and spaniels, on the other hand, absolutely adore travelling. The late eighth Duke of Wellington used to take his black cocker spaniel with him when flying out to his estate in Spain and he told me: 'I was always amused to see him come up on the baggage carousel, happily going along the conveyor belt in his travelling carrier!' On the motorways it is always fun to see all the different breeds of dog with their noses stuck out of the gap in the rear passenger window, taking in what must be a positive rock concert of smells.

It's less amusing though when your own dog is in the back, hyper-salivating and generally very uncomfortable.

The problem is preventable if you start early enough with a young puppy, getting them used to the car and giving them their own special place – preferably a travelling crate – for the journey. Once the travel sickness has set in, it's harder to cure.

First of all, the *Dog Day Diary* is going to be very useful in helping you discover what makes your dog's car sickness better or worse. For example, is it worse at a particular time of day? Or in warm and sunny weather? Or in traffic jams? Or on winding country lanes? Or if he is sitting in the back or the front of the car? All these observations will give you clues about what is causing the dog's discomfort and how to remedy it.

There are also some general ground rules when taking your dog on a car journey, particularly a long one. Firstly, make sure your dog has a proper walk before you set out. A lot of us are under pressure when we're embarking on a long car journey. There's a lot to remember and often the dog just gets chucked in at the last minute before you hit the road at some speed to make up time for being late. Not a good start for a poor-travelling dog. So he needs time to get fresh air and go to the loo. Don't give a main feed until after the journey is over; just a handful of food first thing so that his stomach isn't completely empty.

I always recommend using a good quality travelling pen, preferably fitted in the hatchback. If you have a saloon car then a section of the back seat can hold the pen, safely secured with a strap. There are a number of safety reasons for this, in addition to the dog's comfort. It is compulsory for all human beings to wear seat belts. Most dogs are at least the size of a child, if not bigger. In the event of an accident, tragically, an unsecured dog can become a projectile, flying through the car interior with great force, not only injuring or killing itself but quite possibly, human beings in the car. So even if you have a lovely, quiet dog who always sits uncomplainingly in the passenger foot well, remember that if you are ever unlucky enough to have a serious car accident, the dog won't be able to stop himself flying through the air.

Other, more positive reasons, for using a dog pen relate

to the dog's comfort. I wonder if your children, trying to play on their iPads in the back, ever complain that you're driving 'too swirly' and they're feeling seasick? This goes double for the dog behind them in the hatchback area, sliding back and forth from side to side in the vehicle as you rally drive along a country lane. A sensible size pen with plenty of newspaper or bedding means the dog can bed down and not get thrown about. You can also put his non-spill water bowl in with him and a favourite toy so that it's really just a home from home. Another advantage is that if the dog does throw up, only the pen gets messy. The first few times, just use newspaper to line the pen. Have with you some more newspaper and bin-liners – actually never travel anywhere, with even the most regular of dogs, without newspaper and bin-liners or really, whether you have a dog or not, just take newspaper and bin-liners wherever you go! Anyway, if the dog is sick you can just pull into a service station, dump the messy newspaper straight into the bin-liner, then dump that into the services dog-bin. Put fresh newspaper down and head on for the next few miles!

A good quality dog travelling pen makes for happy journeys.

Always remember to have a back window or quarter-light open when you travel. Fresh air is vital for all animals (including humans). I also have a theory that the very interesting smells carried into the dog help to distract it from its feelings of sickness. With humans it often helps to look at the horizon to counteract seasickness, and I think something similar may happen with dogs, given that their primary sense is smell rather than sight. It wouldn't be surprising if your *Dog Day Diary* shows your dog as more likely to be car sick on a warm, sunny day. To combat this, use your car's air conditioning if fitted. If you don't have air conditioning, keep the car as cool as possible and also use some shading on the rear windows or on the travelling pen, so that direct sunlight doesn't shine on to the dog. You can get temporary shades that are used for travelling with babies and children, and online there are some versions specifically for animal carriage (details at the back of the book).

Poor Coat

While it's natural to blame a dog's poor coat on lack of grooming, please don't beat yourself up about it because in fact there are many reasons why a dog's fur looks lovely and shiny one day and a bit moth-eaten the next. I've included here a picture of my champion stud dog, FTCh Gournaycourt Ginger, looking absolutely glorious. 'In full plumage', as one of my friends calls it. But even he can go through his hearth rug moments!

If your dog is well-fed, well-exercised, happy, healthy and fit it will show in his shiny coat, even if you just flick the brush over it whenever you remember. However, you should groom regularly (I admit I don't do it as often as I should). Look at the website for your dog's breed to get tips on coat management (see the back of the book). Some breeds need specialist grooming due to their long or curling hair. In general I recommend using a wire 'shedding' type brush first to get out any matting or tangles and free up loose hair that needs to be shed, and then finishing off with a bristle brush to smooth the coat and bring up the shine. You can also get grooming gloves that the dogs and I love! Basically you're both enjoying a good old stroke and cuddle at the same time as grooming. In Bristol, stroking an animal is called 'smoothing' it, and that's definitely the right word.

The most important thing when grooming is to use the opportunity for a thorough check of your dog. Check his paws. Are there any grass seeds working their way in between the pads? Any signs of wounds that haven't healed over properly? Certainly nothing should smell nasty. Check his ears. Are they waxy? Are they clogged with dirt? Do they smell? Check his eyes. Are they runny or watering a lot? Check his teeth. There is a type of toothbrush you can get that fits over your finger and makes it a bit easier to clean his teeth (see the back of the book). Having said that, I don't find it at all easy to clean my dogs' teeth. They consider it hilarious and generally squirm about, licking my face and being impossible! You can get various different dental chews and dental-specific foods and I do recommend trying these out. The teeth discussion is one you should have with your vet at the next annual check-up. Most dogs have comparatively bad teeth by the time they are middle-aged, but by working with your vet you can help prevent that. As you are grooming, check the skin under the fur. Make sure there are no lice. These look like little pieces of dandruff, but move if you watch them long enough. Certainly there should be no fleas or ticks! The skin underlying your dog's fur should look smooth and healthy with no little spots, lumps or blemishes.

Sometimes it is possible to overdo the grooming and washing. Many people whose outdoor-style dogs live in the sitting room have to do a lot of dog washing to keep the dog clean enough for polite living. This can result in the dog losing some of the natural oils from his coat and can be a cause of a dry, flaky coat.

Once you've checked all the obvious causes of poor coat while grooming the dog you need to think about elements such as diet. If your dog's poor coat is accompanied by some of the other symptoms listed above, including constantly poor digestion, then food intolerance and sensitivity may be the answer. This could be an allergy to some titbit or other

FTCh Gournaycourt Ginger, 'in full plumage'.

that you regularly give it so cut out all titbits for a while and watch to see if the coat improves. Remember also that hormones play a big part in how your dog's coat looks. After neutering or spaying many dogs lose their lovely shiny coats and their fur becomes much drier and prone to look dull. Entire animals can also get rather patchy coats when their hormones are very active or if they've just had pups. And, of course, there is the dreaded mange! This pesky little parasite lives on foxes and if your dog is an enthusiastic hole explorer there's a small chance it could pick up mange, which causes its fur to fall out in handfuls and is difficult and expensive to cure.

174

Overall, the simplest way to combat a poor coat is through good feeding and a healthy, happy lifestyle for the dog.

Scratching

Scratching and poor coat are very often linked, so do read this section in conjunction with the one above. The most obvious cause of scratching is parasite infestation. As mentioned, ticks, fleas, lice and mange (mites) are the most common parasites that attach themselves to your dog.

Ticks especially need to be taken much more seriously than we did thirty years or so ago, when I first started with dogs. In those days it was comparatively rare for a dog to get a tick, particularly pet dogs and those living in urban or suburban areas. Ticks are carried by sheep, deer and even horses, foxes, hedgehogs and badgers. Nowadays wild deer are much more prevalent throughout the UK, as are badgers. If you don't believe this, sit up quietly one night at two or three o'clock in the morning and you will be very surprised at the animals you see even in quite built-up areas.

Ticks carry a number of parasite-borne diseases that are dangerous for both dogs and humans. The best known of these is Lyme disease, but recently a disease called *Babesiosis*, carried by the tick-borne *Babesia Canis* parasite, has been discovered in the UK, and at least one dog death attributed to it. Nowadays I consider it really essential to have your dog protected from ticks all year round. Your vet will advise on the best method of doing this. One of the problems is that ticks are so tiny that your dog can easily pick one up without you noticing and often the dog doesn't even notice it. The main places you will find ticks attaching are where the fur is thinner – around the belly and tops of the legs and groin, and especially on the nose and head. If one of my dogs picks up a tick most of the time it is on the nose or near the eye. I think this is because the dogs always have their noses in among the grass, sniffing things, which gives the tick an opportunity to climb off the grass stem and on to the dog's nose. Ticks are attracted by body heat and probably carbon dioxide; again, this is more available to the tick where there is less fur. Always check your dog for ticks – particularly if you have been on a country walk. If you find one you should use a special tick remover device (see the back of the book) to twist it out without leaving its mouth parts embedded in the skin. These can cause infections in themselves if left. Even if you have removed the tick successfully, do keep a watch out for any symptoms following a tick bite. For me this is one of the most gruesome bits (not to say bites!) of having a dog, and holding the tick there in the pincers with its legs waving and mandibles chomping is just a horror film!

I would far rather deal with fleas and the rest! If your dog is scratching a lot, fleas, lice or mange are the obvious suspects. A quick check of your dog's coat will usually reveal them. It is something that happens from time to time in the best of dog households. I remember giving a very well-bred pup of mine to a vet and he loved it, but commented: 'It's lousy.' Oh the shame! Ever since then I make sure that any female I'm planning to breed from is well up to date with her anti-parasite programme before mating. I also make sure all the bedding is brand new, as opposed to simply washed (modern low-temperature washes and detergents are simply not up to the job!). The various different anti-parasite products are always being improved, so check what your vet advises and follow the programme carefully.

If the dog is scratching its ears, the cause is usually an ear infection. These can be caused by mites or by foreign bodies such as grass seeds lodging in the ear. Even just a heavy build-up of ear wax can become infected. Dogs with long ear flaps, such as spaniels, are particularly prone to this. A bad smell when you check the ear is a danger signal. Time to go to the vet to get the ear professionally cleansed and some anti-bacterial ear drops prescribed. You should take ear infections very seriously as they can lead to long-term infection, ear drum damage and deafness.

Occasionally scratching can be a symptom of obsessive behaviour. It may be an area where a previous infection or scab has long since heeled, but your dog has got into the habit of scratching it. Or it could be related to a behavioural issue such as displacement activity. Imagine you are having a phone conversation with someone or about something that you would really rather not be doing. You might pick up a biro and doodle, scratch your leg or play with your hair. There's a wonderful example of human displacement activity in the classic black and white film *The Big Sleep*, where Humphrey Bogart catches out Lauren Bacall's character scratching her thigh as their conversation is going against her. So if your dog has a phantom itch, switch over to the section on The Social Problems where you will find more information on this kind of behaviour.

Head Shaking

Usually your dog is shaking its head for the same reason it scratches its ear – because there's an infection or a foreign body lodged or even – just like humans – it's been swimming and got water in its ears. Every dog shakes its head from time to time. Mine tend to give a good old shake when they've been running in long grass or truffling around in the undergrowth. I think this is just a protective mechanism to shake off any bits of leaf or twig, or even perhaps ticks, before they can become firmly stuck. But if head shaking becomes chronic it can be a serious sign. You do need to get your dog checked out by the vet. He may well find an ear problem or perhaps even a tooth abscess, which is fairly easy to deal with. But, very rarely, head shaking or constantly holding the head on one side can be a sign of inherent neurological problems, which you will need veterinary advice about.

Limping/Chewing Paw

One of the things I love about dogs is how generally tough they are. Even the most delicate little handbag-toted

Chihuahua or perfectly groomed poodle is usually a hard-going little nutter when it gets the chance! I have seen my dogs take the most terrible falls and knocks when out on their exercise. Sometimes they end up running full tilt into each other, inflicting tackles that would bring the red card out instantly. Yet, like baggy-shorted 1950s footballers, they soon run it off – something today's Premiership darlings could learn from!

So I don't go into panic mode when I see one of the dogs limping for a while. Even if he's absolutely hopping lame, very often he's just knocked a nerve and has what sportsmen refer to as a dead leg. The leg usually comes back to life long before the end of the walk. What is much more likely to send me into overdrive is persistent chewing on a paw, especially when it's accompanied by a slight limp. This is usually a sign that a grass seed, thorn or other foreign body has got stuck between the pads of the paw and is now working its way in.

Oddly enough, of all the health problems outlined here, this is one of the most serious and likely to become chronic if neglected. Yet frequently it's something that novice owners, obsessing over their dog's runny poo, fail to attend to. I would far rather be dealing with a dog that has the runs than trying to remove all traces of a blackthorn tip wedged in a paw. I had a share in a really good racehorse a while back who was killed by a fragment of blackthorn invisible to the human eye. The structure of a blackthorn causes it to work its way ever deeper into the system, carrying infection into the bloodstream – and in the case of the racehorse, into the very bone marrow.

Check that chewed paw. Even if you can't see anything, bathe it in a weak saline solution at blood heat for at least ten to twenty minutes at a time. Then rinse it with an antiseptic, antibacterial wash such as diluted Hibiscrub before using an antibacterial dusting powder to dry the whole area. Apply a barrier cream or gel (often known among farmers as 'green gunk'), then apply a dressing of sterile cotton wool held in place with a cohesive bandage such as Vetwrap. Then apply a waterproof cover over the top – I often use insulating tape or duct tape or if you live in a farming area you will be able to get hold of silage bag wrap tape. Do all this every day until you are sure all is well. Does this sound like a rigmarole? It is, but it's much less of a performance than trying to cope with a chronic long-term infection that keeps erupting through the top of your dog's paw and could even lead to gangrene. If you're not sure about the dressing routine or how far the foreign body may have got go along to the vet for an initial demonstration.

Hyper-sexual

It was hard to know whether to categorise this issue in the Social Problems section or here as a health issue. In the end I opted to put it here as the most obvious and straightforward solution is veterinary – which is to get your hyper-sexual dog neutered. However, there are important reasons for hyper-sexual behaviour, i.e., mounting everything in sight, commonly known as 'humping your leg syndrome' and immortalised by Mini-Me in Mike Myers's hilarious *Austin Powers: The Spy Who Shagged Me*. In dogs it is really in the spectrum of social maladaptations. It can be a form of dominant behaviour or of displacement activity. Even if your dog is neutered and the hyper-sexual behaviour disappears other problems from the social spectrum may still be present.

Discuss the issue with your vet. Even if you decide to go ahead and have your dog neutered keep a *Dog Day Diary*, which will make you more aware of his behaviour generally. Actions that had not been particularly noticeable because of the need to concentrate on the constant humping may now present their own issue. This is one of the reasons I recommend reading the whole of this book before you get started on solving a particular dog problem. Dog issues are often complex and it can be important to see the whole picture before jumping in on one particular element. So have a look at the Social Problems section and see if that gives you some more insight.

A Note on Veterinary Fees – For obvious reasons, this section of the book often recommends a qualified vet to help you solve your dog's health problems. As you can probably tell, I'm not one for rushing to the vet without good reason. My vet commented the other day that he hadn't seen any of the dogs since the previous year's annual check-up and boosters. Fingers crossed this may long continue.

But there are times when it is vital to get to the surgery, and quickly, and that is not the time to worry about the cost. If you are worried about the fee mention this right from the beginning when you book the dog's appointment. Please don't be embarrassed. Vets are well used to this and most are very helpful about it and can organise solutions. There are also veterinary charities that can help to fund the cost of care and there are details of these at the back of the book.

You may well consider taking out insurance against future veterinary fees. If you have a breed of dog that is well-known for health problems this is certainly worth considering. Also, ask the breed society for your breed if they have any recommendations. Check with dog-owning friends what their experience has been. A friend of mine has an insured dog that developed a chronic infected paw condition (see above) and eventually had to have a series of operations, which were partially covered by her insurance. She told me that by the time she had added up the cost of five years of insurance premiums, her excess and the elements of the treatment not covered by insurance, she was still out of pocket by nearly £2,000. This is purely one person's experience. I'm now feeling very superstitious about writing about dog health at all and I'm just off to double-check all the dogs' paws.

These are the deal-breaker problems that you need to fix, and fix now, before something bad happens. In fact, something bad may already have happened if you are looking at this section. Bear in mind that if your dog is beginning to show aggression or even biting, things are likely to get worse rather than better unless you do something about it – now. The good news is that very often there are obvious and simple solutions to these serious problems, even though the situation may feel scary for you as the dog's Responsible Person. Some issues are harder to deal with, but still definitely solvable. It is quite rare to have to give up on a dog. Be aware though that with the aggression-based group of problems you sometimes have to face facts. In this area, denial is dangerous.

Growling

Animals rarely go nuclear without very good cause. In the wild, confrontation and violence is very risky for an animal. If it is injured it could very well die from its wounds. Even if it is successful in its action, other animals may have taken the opportunity to rush in behind the fighter's back and attack other members of the pack or herd – or have sex with them for that matter! A study of the 'rut' of male red stags in Scotland showed that the champion stag, with a massive rack of antlers, fighting all comers, actually got less sex and spread his genes less widely than the weedier stags mooching round the edge of the herd not getting involved. I have to say that the human comparison to this is absolutely unavoidable! You can't help thinking of all those chaps just popping round while hubby's away, 'Oh, don't worry about me, I'm a lover not a fighter ...'

With so much at stake, most animals, of whatever species, will give plenty of warning and go through lots of different stages of arousal before actually attacking. There will be posturing and vocalisation and body language and false charging. It's all designed to create a stand-off and allow both parties to more or less back down before any real damage is done. If you watch animal behaviour in the wild, or on the Discovery Channel, you will see an awful lot of posturing, but not all that much genuine action. It's a bit like a classic Saturday night pub brawl, with both parties yelling: 'Hold me back, lads! Hold me back!'

I think of growling as being very much that stage of the argument. In a sense, the dog is being almost the opposite of aggressive. In humans, you might consider it to be at the negotiating phase of a row. The dog is at least bothering to communicate that it has an issue and giving fair warning that a potential problem could arise. Something or someone is pressing its buttons, and rather than rushing to war the dog is giving both sides a chance to calm things down.

You should mirror this behaviour as far as possible. Think John F. Kennedy and the Cuban missile crisis! At this stage you have a chance to back off, without backing down. So first of all take the dog out of the situation that caused the growling. If your dog is off the lead, then get him back on the lead. Standing slightly behind and to one side of him, use a loop-lead to slip over his head. Try not to 'get in his face' and confront him while you are putting him back on the lead and, just in case, don't get your hands too near his mouth. A lot of dogs will be much calmer the moment they are on the lead. It helps give them a feeling of boundaries and takes the pressure out of a situation.

The big thing you can do at this stage is to avoid escalating things. So don't try to be over-dominant with your dog and start yelling at him or being physical. He hasn't done that yet, and neither should you. At this point you are probably not even 100 per cent sure why he is behaving in this way. A major cause of anger and aggression, in both animals and humans, is fear-based, rather than a genuine desire to be violent. So don't try to 'stare down' your dog by forcing eye contact on him as you might simply make him more intimidated. Get your dog into his safe place, usually his indoor pen at home, and settle him with a chew or toys so he can calm down and get back to normal.

Take the opportunity to spend some time quietly assessing the situation. Has he done this before? If so, create a retrospective *Dog Day Diary* to try to get a full picture of when, where and why he growls. If this is the first time he's done it, think carefully about the situation that led up to his growling. Were you somewhere different? Was he growling at you, someone else or at another dog? Had he met the other dog before? Is your dog female? Might she be in season? We can all get a bit hormonal at times! What might have changed? Carefully check other sections of this book. The most relevant are 'timid' in the Endearing Problems section and generally the Social Problems section. Importantly, you should also check out the Health-Related Problems section. If a dog that is normally good-tempered suddenly starts growling when you want to groom it, immediately suspect some kind of pain issue.

Older dogs are also prone to become rather growly and aggressive towards the end of their lives, especially with other dogs. Sometimes this can be because the dog has become rather blind or deaf without us really noticing it. Because a dog's primary sense is that of smell, it can be surprisingly hard to realise from day to day that another of the dog's senses is failing. But when an older dog is confronted with a dog that it can smell but not really see very well, it's very likely to feel as if it is in a risky or threatening situation. A visit to the vet is a good place to start if your dog suddenly becomes a bit growly.

Another important element to determine is whether the dog is growling at you or at something else. If he's growling at you it could be because you are unintentionally doing something that is giving him pain. Or you may be causing him to feel threatened or pressurised – and it can be very hard to work out what you could possibly be doing! Sometimes it is something very simple, like you trying to take away his favourite toy, and this is dealt with under 'possessive' in the section. But you may be absolutely baffled as to why your dog is growling at you! Keep the pressure off your dog while you are using your *Dog Day Diary* to do your detective work. Most of the time you will be able to spot some slight change, usually in the dog's social situation, that has put him off his 'A-game'. If that change can't be rectified then he will need some empathy from you and probably the chance to have distractions to take his mind off things. A friend of mine recently converted what had been the children's play room into a granny pad. Because the dog's pen was in the play room it had to be moved and this was when the dog's growling started. Obviously moving the dog's pen back was not an option! So in this case my friend watched closely to see where the dog seemed most comfortable round the house and then gradually moved its feeding and eventually its pen to that spot.

If your dog is growling at other dogs or people it meets out and about you may not feel as if you have so much control over the situation, but don't worry, there are plenty of things you can do! The first thing is to work out whether the dog's growling is coming from a place of timidity/fear or of dominance/genuine aggression.

When you look closely at the situation, and check through your *Dog Day Diary*, the answer to that question is likely to be obvious. If fear/anxiety/timidity/insecurity is at the heart of the growling then you can take the measures described here and elsewhere in the book. You need to be supportive of your dog and become a bit of a psycho-dog-analyst. Don't try to prevent your dog from growling. Remember, this is his JFK moment and he is using his growling to bring his world back from the brink of atomic war. Deny him this coping mechanism and he could end up with nowhere else to go but push the nuclear button.

A coping mechanism is a behaviour adopted by any animal (including humans) to help them cope with a situation they find extremely stressful. These coping mechanisms often appear to be quite negative; in a dog they can be seen as 'bad behaviour'. We are probably all familiar with human coping mechanisms such as drinking too much or the third chocolate chip muffin. Dogs have similar coping mechanisms (including the Chocolate-chip Muffin Mechanism). Some of these are known as 'displacement activities' and are discussed in the Social Problems section. With your dog, it is important to recognise when his behaviour is coming from a coping mechanism, as growling often does. As a society we tend to be very dismissive of coping mechanisms, whether we find them in animals or humans. The alcoholic is stigmatised for his or her drinking without anyone ever really bothering to find out what it might be that could be so bad that being an alcoholic is a better option. So, rather than trying to deny your dog his coping mechanism, get to the bottom of what it is he is trying to cope with.

Using some kind of muzzle or other physically restraining bit of kit is not a good idea as it simply suppresses the problem without solving it. Show some respect for your dog. He's a living animal, not a machine, and it needs your personal engagement to help fix him, not a screwdriver. The only bit of kit I might use is the 'dog in training' tabard, so that other people can understand you are working on your dog's issue.

Rarely, your dog's growling may be coming from a place of dominance and aggression. This kind of growling can escalate into actual aggression, which is discussed next.

Aggressive with Other Dogs

So there's been a bit of a dust up in the park. The first thing to do is take a deep breath and go gently. When dogs lose the plot with each other, the chances are that their humans will, too! Do not get involved in a furious row with the owner of the other dog about who started it. You will want to answer that question in due course, privately, at home. Now is not the time to step in with a full-on gypsy-style defence of your dog – tempting though it may be! Apologise (who cares, it's only words), and as quietly and as quickly as possible, remove your dog and yourself from the situation.

It is surprising how much and how often the human owner's feelings contribute to the dog's behaviour towards other dogs. My dog, Dutch, was a strong, handsome spaniel. Possibly, if you were being hyper-critical you might say that in an ideal world he was maybe, perhaps, just a tad headstrong, even wild. I wouldn't recommend anyone actually saying such a thing about Dutch in my presence. The proverb goes: You can criticise a man's job, his house, even his wife – but you must never say a word against his dog. Anyway, one of the other ladies in my social circle had a large, dim and particularly useless, but fashionable, flatcoat retriever. Dutch and the retriever despised each other. Their mutual lack of respect often tipped over into some fairly aggressive posturing. However! There is no doubt that both dogs considered themselves fully entitled to their behaviour, since it has to be admitted that their two owners felt pretty much the same about each other at a human level as the dogs did at a canine level. The dogs were simply acting out a psychological dynamic that was going on between their owners. It used to make the rest of our human gang laugh to hear us telling off our dogs. 'Oh Dutch, oh dear, did you just happen to grab him by the throat? Oh my, what a pity, bad boy, never mind ...'

So, when you have got back home and put the kettle on, it is time to consider who started it. Was it your dog? Was it the other dog? Was it the other lady? Was it you? Of course, you will initially be convinced that it was the other dog, or possibly the lady, who was wearing a particularly ghastly pair of pink polka dot wellies. But now you must be honest. Has this kind of thing happened before? Do you see that lady quite often in the park in her ridiculous wellies? Was your dog the first to get stuck in? Were you reluctant to step off the path to let the other lady past with her stupid dog and her silly wellies? Were you in a particularly foul mood that morning? Was the other lady clearly in a bad temper already, and not giving you time to get off the path?

You need to be absolutely truthful about how the

aggression came into the situation and from where. If it was just a one-off, and you can honestly answer that neither your dog – nor you – was feeling aggressive or ready to kick-off, that's great news. Just avoid that particular situation in future. Walk the dog at a different time of day or on a different route. Or if you see Pink Welly Woman coming, hide behind a bush!

But if this kind of thing keeps happening, and for one reason or another your dog always seems to be getting into confrontations, then it is time to take responsibility. You are the dog's owner, and you have to own the problem, for both you and the dog. As usual, start by keeping your *Dog Day Diary*. While you are gathering your information be sure to exercise your dog in a safe place and go out of your way to avoid possible confrontations. Now check out your diary. Remember my diary at the beginning of the book? My dog problem then wasn't aggression related, but the diary helped me to realise that my dog problems, of any kind, tend to crop up when I am feeling stressed for some reason. Have a look at your diary. It wouldn't be at all surprising to find that your dog's aggressive behaviour is worse on days when you are in a bit of a tizz yourself.

In busy dog-walking areas, particularly some of the London commons, a new phenomenon has been noticed. You could call it 'lead rage'. It is the canine equivalent of road rage, where dog walkers are stomping round the common or park, getting into rows with other dog walkers about poo-picking and all manner of things. It's already well known that if you are driving when very stressed or upset you are more likely to experience an accident or an incident of road rage – even if it's not you that causes it. So, if your diary is pointing up some unsettling truths, take a step back. Dogs instinctively pick up on human mood and body language, so his apparent bad behaviour may actually be telling you something about yourself. Being with your dog should be one of the best bits in your day, but if life has reached the point where even that is stressful or not enjoyable then maybe you need to take a tip from Lassie and get help.

If you have genuinely reached the conclusion that it wasn't you who started it or the other dog, or even Pink Welly Woman, but definitely your own dog, then still don't panic; there's plenty that can be done. As is so often the case, the first thing to think about is sex. If your dog is a female it is very likely that she will get snappy when she is feeling hormonal, which usually happens twice a year for about three to four weeks including all phases. A dog sniffing her backside at the wrong moment is likely to get a considerable flea in its ear. Although, of course, at the right moment, which usually lasts about three or four days, the male could find himself running for cover for an entirely different reason! If you want to breed from your female read up about the oestrus cycle and accept the fact that she will have to go into purdah a couple of times a year. If you don't want to breed from her the spaying operation is worth considering. Have a chat with your vet about it. The vet is likely to be quite supportive as it can prevent certain cancers in later life. The downside is that your female dog may gain weight more easily and her coat could become dull.

You should also have the conversation about neutering if you have a male dog. When they become fully mature around the age of eighteen months to two years old, depending on breed, many male dogs do develop dominance and aggression issues related to their sex hormones. They can also be a big nuisance with female dogs, whether the female is in season or not. A young male dog of mine constantly sniffs one of the females, even though she has been spayed. I have told him he's barking up the wrong tree, but as she seems to find it rather flattering the situation is fine. If your male dog is hyper-sexual and this is giving him social problems have a conversation with the vet. I wouldn't recommend breeding from him in any case unless he has proved himself to be an outstanding example of his breed. Forgive me for making an assumption, but I'm guessing that, since you're reading this book, this probably isn't the case no matter how wonderful he may be in other ways.

Another, more complex, cause of aggression towards other

dogs is if your dog cannot speak Dog. Dogs communicate with each other in all sorts of ways. They can vocalise by growling, barking, whining, whimpering, howling and even singing. They can emote through body language and facial expression. They probably have a very highly developed language of smell that we humans can't perceive. Most dogs learn enough of this language during puppyhood and in later socialisation so that they can communicate easily with dogs that are strangers to them. Two or more dog households especially tend to raise dogs that are 'clubbable' and socialise easily with other dogs. Mind you, the dog family can be pretty rough and ready sometimes. I have this fantasy idea that my dogs, living and adventuring together all these years, will love each other deeply. Observing them when they don't know I'm there, I've been rudely awakened. Most of the time they seem just to ignore each other. Occasionally there's a bit of a row over something. There's certainly nothing lovey-dovey going on, but there are genuine bonds. After dinner each evening they all sing together. It's quite sweet seeing them with their noses in the air, ears trailing backwards and round mouths going: 'Woooo, wooooo, woooo'. The other moment you realise that they were actually true friends is when one old dog finally goes to Rabbit In Peace and his kennel-mate of the same age often follows not long after. The rest of the time, they're like any family, not giving each other the time of day.

Being with your dogs should be one of the best bits of your day.

nigeburrphotography.co.uk

But they can certainly speak Dog. I think the rough and tumble of the canine family gives them all the communication skills they need to use when meeting strange dogs. If the strange dog comes on a bit strong, well my dogs have seen it all before at home. They don't take it to heart. Whatever the canine equivalent is of a grin, a slap on the back and a friendly laugh seems to be how a dog-socialised dog is able to defuse situations.

Today though, fewer of us have the luxury of having more than one dog. Most dogs are raised as only dogs, and many don't come across other dogs that often. Add to this a tendency for their human owners to treat them like humans and you can end up with a dog that doesn't speak much Dog, and may not even realise it is a dog. Many currently fashionable breeds of dog also tend to have very small litter sizes and may occasionally have to be hand-reared, giving them even less opportunity to actualise themselves as a dog.

Increasingly, I am seeing dogs in which all these difficulties are combining. The dog has been born into comparative isolation in its puppyhood and then finds itself as an only dog in a home where it is actually treated like a human, being allowed to sleep in the human bed, etc. This dog is at a real disadvantage when it eventually meets other dogs. It can speak only a few words of the language and probably doesn't even really consider itself to be a dog. So when the other dog tests it out a little, maybe just messing around or even a bit of wind-up, the only dog just doesn't have the socialisation or communication skills to take it safely through the situation. All sorts of behaviours can result. Very often the only dog will quickly be aggressive because it simply doesn't have the personal resources to deflect the issues or shrug things off. And there is often some trigger in the only dog's body language – which will be faulty from a social dog's point of view – that causes the only dog to spark incidents. Even in the human world we can all recognise that person who somehow just doesn't get it right and always seems to rub people up the wrong way for reasons we can't explain.

Consider this aspect of your dog's behaviour very carefully. If you have friends with more than one dog, have a chat with them about the way their dogs live, compared with the way your only dog lives. The best solution is to teach your dog to speak Dog. You may have to take some responsibility if you have admitted to yourself that you treat him too much as a human. Equally important is to get him out there meeting

nice, friendly, helpful dogs in a controlled situation – which will be the local dog obedience class. You can go online to find these, but personally I prefer to start by chatting with your vet or an experienced friend who will be able to put you in touch with the right local class.

It may look like they're ignoring each other, but these three are 'talking Dog' all the same.

Case History: Joe's Well-Socialised Working Dogs

As a farrier and countryside vermin controller, Joe's dogs are workers as well as companions. As well as enjoying all sorts of outdoor activities with Joe, they meet a lot of other dogs in day-to-day life. They are well-socialised so can enjoy play with new dogs. But, as you can see, their bond with Joe is very strong, and a word from him will keep them close by his side when needed.

(Above) Joe and his team setting out for work.

(Right) Joe's dogs meet up with Ricky.

Chasing and Worrying Other Animals

This issue is included here under the **Serious Problems** category because it is indeed a very serious problem – one that could, at worst, result in your dog being legally destroyed. It is illegal for a dog to chase or worry sheep or other livestock, and if your dog does this persistently the police may get involved and your dog could be taken away from you. And yet, unlike most of the other issues in this section, it is not really an aggression spectrum problem. It is much more related to natural canine behaviour that has not been successfully modified. It is an instinctive behaviour for most dogs to chase almost anything that moves, from a rolling tennis ball to next door's cat to a baby lamb. Some types of dog have been selectively bred for hundreds, if not thousands of years, to encourage this behaviour. These breeds and types include not just those we associate with herding or chasing, such as sheepdogs, but also hounds, Labrador retrievers, spaniels, corgis, Dalmatians, Rottweilers and even terriers.

Really almost all our current 'pet' dogs of medium size and upwards originally had working roles that involved some degree of chasing or herding. Even the Queen's famous corgis get their tendency to nip the occasional ankle of a visiting foreign dignitary from their original role of 'heeler' dogs, who would round up cattle and sheep by running in and snapping at the animals' legs. Dalmatians, everybody's favourite 'designer dog', were originally kept to run at the back of a horse-drawn carriage and ward off any undesirable human who tried to jump aboard to get a ride or to steal. That slender little whippet curled up by the telly was once used by poachers to hunt hares and rabbits for the pot. With dogs such as bloodhounds, wolfhounds, deerhounds, German shepherds, etc, the clue is in the name. Dachs, for example, is German for badger. So keep in mind that your comical looking sausage-dog dachshund was originally used in Germany to hunt badgers – something that is illegal now. With Labrador retrievers, the most popular breed of dog in the Western world, it pays to understand what the word 'retriever' means. Millions of Labrador retrievers are still working all over the world today in their original role of chasing, capturing and bringing back birds and animals that have been wounded by shooters. Working retrievers are trained to do this only on command, and they are also taught the difference between injured and uninjured animals. Pet retrievers don't usually get that kind of training, but the instinct doesn't go away.

All these dogs, including mine and yours, will probably chase something at some point. Nobody has told their DNA that this is no longer desirable behaviour. And actually, I would have less respect for a dog that didn't have the moxie to make a determined effort to chase at least next door's cat every now and then. Even multiple field trial champion Gournaycourt Ginger (yes, the one who collects the dishes) has had a good old chase or two during his distinguished career.

The problem lies in what, when, how and why your dog chases. If he chases a tennis ball, fine, that's a game, and part of some great training exercises. If he chases birds, that's still not too much of a problem, but some training would be helpful. But if he chases newborn lambs or calves, or a protected species such as a hare or badger, that is a big problem. When does he chase? If it's just once in a while, when temptation proves too much, again you can deal with that. But if he chases obsessively, all the time, whenever he gets a chance, you have a really difficult issue. And how is he chasing? Is it just a half-hearted, saw it move, go for it, give up? That's how most dogs chase and it can be easily corrected. Full-on chasing, which is deliberate and determined, and doesn't stop until the dog has actually caught the lamb, is very likely to end up with the removal and possible destruction of the dog. The final, really important, question, is why he chases. If he just couldn't help himself this once and you didn't call him back in time, fair enough, you'll just have to be a bit quicker and more alert. But if he is chasing and worrying animals because he is completely out of control and has no respect for you or anything else, then this is more or less at the terminal end of the chasing behaviour spectrum. That is truly a psycho dog I'm afraid.

Ask yourself all these questions and answer them honestly. You don't have to tell anyone else the answer! But you do need to be aware of all these factors if you are going to solve the problem of your dog chasing. For the owners of urban dogs the issue of chasing is usually less of a pressing problem than it is for rural dog owners. That doesn't mean it can be ignored. There is a surprisingly large amount of wildlife in towns and suburbs. A wander around your local park in the early hours of the morning may reveal badgers, rabbits and roe deer as well as foxes, cats and drunks. Birds, ponies and squirrels are everywhere and, of course, there are other dogs. On any number of levels you don't want your dog chasing any of these. In some cases it is illegal. It can lead to unpleasant incidents and it can also put your dog in danger, particularly if he ends up running out into a road while chasing. Also, you may want to take your urban dog into the countryside for walks or on country holidays. Then he will be tempted by lots more animals including poultry, gamebirds such as pheasants, hares, sheep, lambs, cattle, goats, llamas and, of course, the inevitable deer, badgers, ponies, cats, rabbits, foxes, squirrels, etc. Really, the countryside is absolutely heaving with temptation for your dog to chase!

Many country families use aversion therapy on their dogs at a young age. There will be a local animal – often an old female cow or sheep – that is known to give as good as it gets. The young dog will be allowed to chase it and very quickly learn its error! A West Country friend had the dreaded Ramkin, an elderly ram with anger management issues. Many a young dog would come flying back over the hedge assisted by Ramkin's horns. This isn't always successful or appropriate. If you have a dog that you do want to work, perhaps in country sports, you don't want him so put off chasing that he can't do his job.

In some cases the aversion method doesn't work anyway.

When I was recovering from yet another sports injury, Hugh had the job of exercising the dogs, including Dutch, a working dog who had what I consider to be an admirably high drive. Walking across a local field, Hugh noticed the farmer had put out his geese to graze. Unfortunately Dutch had spotted this a few seconds earlier and was already zooming across the field in determined pursuit of the flock of geese. Hugh thought: ah geese, dangerous, bad-tempered birds, they will turn on Dutch and he will soon be running back with his tail between his legs. Not a bit of it. Dutch turned out to be more than a match for the geese. By the time Hugh had caught up with him, he already had one separated from the flock, and who knows what might have happened next!

I suppose I always was a little in denial about Dutch's faults. However, I bit the bullet on that one and taught him not to chase. So your first solution is to come out of denial and accept that your dog does have a problem, and that you need to do something about it now, before it's too late. Often all that's needed is some obedience training along the lines described in the Irritating Problems section. You can also find a lot more detail about how to apply this out in the countryside in *Training the Working Spaniel*. However, sometimes these methods can be quite difficult for a novice to learn, and with so much at stake it would be a good idea to get help. The obedience class route may be useful and is certainly easy to access. But in this instance, where you have a real country problem, a country sports solution may be best. Find a professional working dog trainer or a working dog training club and seek their assistance. The Kennel Club has various contacts for trainers and clubs. Going online is also helpful. You can put the breed of your dog into the search engine and you will come up with lots of useful and relevant results.

While you are getting this sorted out you must keep your dog out of trouble. From now on I'm afraid your stroll in the park is no longer going to be 'a stroll in the park'! Be aware of anything that he might chase long before he is. Don't let him be like Dutch and spot the geese before you do. You can't wander along planning your next night out with the girls. You must be alert and concentrate on your job of exercising the dog. Use a lead or flexi-lead wherever necessary. If you are confronted by someone accusing your dog of chasing do not start an argument; remove your dog and yourself from the situation as quickly as possible. You are not on good legal ground. As I write this I have just returned from exercising my dogs on my own private area, where one of my dogs was chased and nipped by a collie and a lurcher, whose owner was actually trespassing. I filmed this on my mobile while the dogs' owner ranted and swore at me. These are pressured situations for all concerned, so you need to take responsibility to prevent things escalating, no matter what your own feelings are. This is important for your dog's sake as much as anything. The majority of cases that I have experienced, where a dog has eventually been removed or even destroyed, have reached that point only because of the owner's stubborn refusal to co-operate with the other parties involved in the matter. No animal owner ever wants to see another animal destroyed and if it gets that far it is because they have been pushed, so don't be the one to push it.

Bad with Visitors/Guarding

It can feel very flattering to have a dog that is possessive and protective of you, guarding you from all-comers! If you have one of the herding or guarding breeds of dog, it is likely that a certain amount of protective behaviour may develop as the dog grows up. These breeds have been genetically selected over the generations to protect animals and humans from external attack, and that DNA doesn't disappear just because you don't have any sheep or because you are unlikely to be attacked at any moment by a horde of rampaging Vikings, exciting as that might be! It can, however, be quite handy if you are a female who goes running alone, or perhaps if your home is in an area with a high rural crime rate. The downside is when the dog starts exhibiting the behaviour inappropriately or with aggression. The *Psycho Spectrum* shows how there is a risk of endearing, almost Lassie-type behaviour, escalating into a dog that won't let your mates stop to chat with you or won't allow visitors into the house. Right at the very beginning, look at the website for the specific breed or breed-type of your dog. The quickest way is to go to the Kennel Club website, www.thekennelclub.org.uk, and have a look at the section covering your breed. An alternative is Discover Dogs, www.discoverdogs.org.uk, which aims to introduce owners to all the different breeds. Knowing a little about your breed will help you with what to expect. Obviously, the best time to take all this on board is while your dog is still a puppy, so there is plenty of information about this in *From Puppy to Perfect*. By now though, your dog is already grown up and clearly exhibiting enough of these tendencies to cause you concern.

With your overprotective dog, keep your *Dog Day Diary* for a while to see if you can pinpoint any particular occasions when its behaviour cuts in. That might give rise to a few hard questions which it is not within the scope of this book to answer. For example, is the dog well justified in its view that you need protecting? And why? I'm sure you've heard the joke 'it's me or the dog' – but isn't that really rather a controlling remark? And might the dog be very well aware of its precarious position in the household? Perhaps human beings need to sit down and have a chat first. There is a lot more discussion of this issue in the Social Problems section that you may find interesting.

Start a gradual process of allowing your dog to realise that you and it are both in a secure situation and that you are not mutually dependent. Recruit a friend to help you at first. Set up a dog pen or run in your friend's garden. On your own, take your dog to it and put him in there with some food and water. If he is not possessive with toys, but only with you, put some of his toys in with him. Leave him there while you go indoors to meet your friend. I recommend having a coffee together somewhere that you can watch the dog without being seen by him – maybe out of the kitchen window.

When the dog is really relaxed and settled with his toys and has had something to eat, you stay where you are, watching. Your friend goes out to the dog and quietly offers him a treat, slips the lead on and takes him for a wander round before putting him back in the pen. Then your friend goes back indoors and when the dog settles again you go out on your own, praise the dog and take it back home.

You can't perform this exercise anywhere that the dog considers to be its territory or where it can still see you otherwise it will continue to be in protective mode. It's important to let the dog have a period of detachment first before your friend comes out. But you need to be somewhere you can see what is happening so that you can go out and end the lesson if necessary.

If your dog is reasonably calm with other dogs, it is worth considering a good quality boarding kennels for a week. You are trying to offer the dog a space where it can feel the pressure is off. You aren't around, so the heavy responsibility of protecting you is eased, and the dog can have a chance to chill and be itself for a while. It is stressful constantly being on your guard, so you aim to get the dog into less stressful situations. Once the dog has relaxed enough that you and he can go out safely in public then group dog training classes can work really well.

Biting/Aggressive with Humans

This is really the Mount Everest of dog problems. From a training point of view it is the peak of them all and appears insurmountable. But Everest has foothills and base camp and a number of other points on the climb. It is the same with your dog and his aggression or biting. The summit of the problem – the actual bite or attack – has been arrived at by many stages. Sometimes the owner may be more or less unaware, or perhaps in denial, of these different levels, but they will certainly have been there. Very few dogs come into this world with a primary intention to attack human beings.

I have left this problem until the last section of the chapter because I hope that by this time you will have read through lots of discussion of the behaviour spectrum and the *Psycho Tree* and looked at various related issues. This will have given you a better understanding of how unwanted behaviour arises in our dogs. It really helps to have a broad picture of what is going on. Not only does it give you tremendous insight into why your dog is being aggressive, but this knowledge very often provides you with an instinctive solution to the problem in your particular case.

Equipped with your reading, you can take a view about whether your dog's bite or sudden aggression may be a one-off caused by pain, discussed earlier. You will have discovered the way timidity and fear in a dog can flip over into an unexpected attack. You should also have a good idea of where your particular dog's behaviour fits in on the band that includes growling, guarding and possessiveness. We've also discussed the role that socialisation plays in a dog's behaviour both towards other dogs and towards humans.

But if you have got to this final section and still need to read on then it may be that your dog's problem is coming from a place of genuine aggression, as opposed to behaviour triggered by other underlying issues. It is rare for a dog to be naturally aggressive, even if it is an alpha-type dog with a high drive and responsibility motivation. Usually these 'pack-leader' dogs have canine/human social skills and intelligence that allow them to socialise easily, so they can assert themselves where necessary without the need to be aggressive. Some breeds of dog are considered to be more prone to aggression than others, but again, professional handlers and most owners of these breeds will tell you that they are rarely initially aggressive, although they may be more easily trained to display aggressive behaviours than other breeds.

Most dogs that bite or attack have been trained to do so by their owners – either deliberately or accidentally. Some owners like to play mouthing, biting, tugging and chewing games with their puppies from the outset. But really this is the time you should be teaching your pup that mouthing and biting is not encouraged. Give your pup specialist chew toys for its teething stages. As it grows up it can move on to adult chews and there will always be a clear distinction between its toy that can be chewed and human hands that cannot. Tugging games teach your young dog how to lock its jaws. That, again, is not something you want to encourage in family life.

Don't be fooled into thinking your dog bit you 'by mistake'. Dogs are every bit as well aware of what they have in their mouths as humans are and, just like us, they use their tongues to sort out what can be bitten: the cherry, from what can't: the cherry stone. I can hold an ice cream lolly for my dogs to finish off, which they do just like us humans, by licking, leaving the stick perfectly intact. So if the dog nipped your fingers, he knew it!

By the time the biting/aggression issue has reached the Mount Everest stage, it is time to look at the whole difficult area of dominance. We've discussed dogs that show dominance towards other dogs and this arises from their degree of canine socialisation. When the biting is directed towards a human, the dog's dominance stems from a breakdown in the bond between the dog and its owner, or to an incorrect bond having formed. This process starts from the moment the puppy or dog arrives in the house. Watching how this works between a group of dogs gives a good insight into where things can go wrong when the dog is living solely with humans, as opposed to living with both dogs and humans. When I breed a litter of puppies there is always a slightly tense stage when all the puppies have been weaned and mum has rejoined the rest of the dogs, but a pup that I have retained isn't quite old enough to join in with the gang. This is particularly because the mum, with the best will in the world, couldn't care less if she never saw the pup again after all that time of not just feeding it, but also eating its poo! Soon the pup will be old enough to join in with everybody else, but you need to introduce it quite carefully.

No matter how tactful you are about the process, the

day of 'The Bite' will occur. 'The Bite' is the moment when the main adult dog in the group considers that not only has the pup got out of its box a step too far, but also it is old enough to be chastised. Hence, The Bite. The dogs sort this out for themselves and there's not much we humans can do about it other than disinfect the wound with a weak solution of Hibiscrub or similar. I didn't breed Ricky myself, but collected him from his breeders when he was about ten weeks. He was a young dog of around five months old when it happened that the breeders were dropping round for tea. I was so looking forward to showing off young Ricky to them and demonstrating how well he was doing in his training work. Unfortunately this had to be the day that Ricky decided he was a grown-up, cheeked the top dog and received The Bite. By the time I went to get him to be groomed, his nose had gone up like a balloon and he looked more like the loser in a fight with Mike Tyson than a handsome young spaniel. The swelling went down in a couple of days and everything was back to normal. Once administered, The Bite never happens again. But it had to be that one day when I wanted him to look his best!

In canine terms, The Bite is the moment when overly dominant behaviour is quite literally nipped in the bud. As humans we need to be able to do something similar with a dog that has an attitude problem. You could even consider administering The Bite yourself, as old school professional dog trainers used to do, but I wouldn't recommend the idea of getting a mouthful of fur! So we need to work out other ways of showing our boundary-pushing youngster that his dominant behaviour will not be tolerated. Don't be too concerned to do this very early on. Remember how dogs work it between themselves. The Bite never happens straight away, but only when the whippersnapper is old enough to learn from it. If you go around being overly dominant and repressive with a young puppy it will become timid and fearful – increasing the chances of the problem developing that you were trying to prevent in the first place.

A reader had a fairly lengthy correspondence with

me recently about his cocker spaniel puppy that he was concerned had dominance issues. His initial question was about which type of harness to buy because he was worried the puppy would be pulling on the lead. I suggested that some simple heel-work lessons would be more suitable, which was when I discovered that the puppy was only ten weeks old. At this point the reader mentioned his concerns about aggression and dominance problems he was having with the pup. At ten weeks old a cocker spaniel puppy is still small enough to sit in the palm of a man's cupped hands. I suddenly had a mental picture of this puppy dominating my reader, and I must admit it was really hard to address the problem with the degree of seriousness my reader felt it warranted. However, we got there! I was able to let my reader understand that he could relax and just enjoy his time with the young pup. Personally, I realised that it is all too easy to read lots of stuff online about dominance and get very anxious about whether you are doing the right thing, so it was a learning curve for both of us.

Take a tip from the canine point of view and let yourself know instinctively when the moment has come to assert yourself. With many youngsters you will never really need to do it as they may not be very ambitious about their status. But with high-drive, motivated juniors, the moment may come. If the puppy is still young or small enough, you can scruff it. Grab it firmly and none-too-gently by the scruff of the neck and lift it right up off all its paws. I like to hold mine at eye level, but not too close to my face, so that I can safely eyeball it at the same time as giving it a good telling off and shaking it a bit. This is the human equivalent of The Bite, and it says unequivocally: 'What are you thinking of you little hoodlum. The boss is on top here. Look I can pick you right up with just one hand, so think on ...' Most pups get the message straight away. No animal likes to lose control in this way and your physical power, mental determination and willingness to use it is clearly demonstrated to the youngster.

If the dog is a bit older, or from one of the larger breeds, making it too heavy to pick up and scruff in this way, you can still 'take it off its paws'. Standing to one side and slightly behind your dog (always keep your own face out of harm's way when demonstrating physical superiority), slip your arms under the armpits of your dog's front legs. You can link your hands in front of its chest if you want. Now lift it right off its front legs at the same time as giving it a good verbal ticking off. Dogs hate not being able to move their front legs. The whole thing is quite demeaning, even for a biggish dog, and proves to it that you can get full-on if need be.

There is another technique I use with a dog that is being a bit of a nuisance. It is handy if the dog might be particularly muddy or wet and I don't want to get any more wet and muddy than I usually am. With a welly boot-clad foot, place your boot firmly on the point between the dog's shoulder blades and press down so the dog has no alternative but to go down, and some will even roll over and show their belly at this point. You can hold them down with your foot for a few seconds, asserting yourself still further. The dog knows you have forced it into this submissive position and quickly realises that dominance is not an option for it.

All these techniques are the human equivalent of The Bite. They are decisive, firm and fair. Crucially, you must pick your moment to administer this display of your dominance. The young dog should be old enough to know what it is doing and to realise that it has failed. Don't back down or dither. Decide: the next time the dog does that, I'm taking action. Be ready and when and if the dog is overly dominant again, do what you have planned. When done at the right time in the adolescent dog's life you will probably never need to do it again. None of my young dogs has ever been bitten twice! However, with dogs where biting and aggression has become an issue that moment has usually passed and the dog is already too set in his ways for The Bite to be sufficient.

This usually happens in households where The Bite, or its human equivalent, has never taken place. I find it most often in homes where boundaries have not been set and the dog has never been given any firm guidelines about its behaviour. Check out the Social Problems section for more discussion on how this can cause a range of problems. If you are in this situation you will need to start changing your attitude to the dog and your routines with it. Some behaviourists recommend muzzling the dog from the start and you may have to consider this if your dog interacts with the public a great deal. However, if your dog's temperament has become unreliable it would be best to avoid those type of situations until you have got a handle on the problem. In fact, most biting and aggression takes place in the home with family members. So I would tend to keep a pair of heavy gardening gloves at the ready rather than rushing to buy a muzzle. For one thing, you do eventually have to take the muzzle off again – and who knows what might happen at that delicate moment!

Instead you must set about teaching your dog some boundaries, which should be a gradual process. It is unfair suddenly to throw a whole bunch of rules at a dog that has never had any before. Begin by reducing the number of places and ways in which he can be physically dominant.

Remember, a dog at eye level or higher with a human considers itself to be one up on a human. In order to gain eye level, most dogs would have to stand on a box. And who has given them the box to stand on? Yes, you did! If you let a dominant dog sit up on the back of the sofa or sleep on the bed, you are putting it at eye level to humans.

Use your *Dog Day Diary* to journal the situations and places where the dog might feel dominant. If it is allowed the

Even if you didn't use a pen when your dog was a puppy, definitely use it if you are having any issues.

nigeburrphotography.co.uk

run of the sitting room where humans are sitting down, it will quickly get the idea of being on a par or above a human. Is it allowed in the dining room while you are sitting down eating? Is it allowed to nick titbits from the human dinner table? All these things encourage a dog to feel entitled in its dominance. Become well aware of the moments when your dog is prone to aggression and work out what else is happening at the time, and where he is.

From behind or to the side at a distance is a safe approach to removing an object from a dog's mouth – don't encourage a tug of war.

A good bracing position if a dog seems ready to attack.

If your dog doesn't have an indoor pen, you really must introduce one. Make it a nice place for the dog to be. Feed him in there. It separates him physically, literally and metaphorically from the humans. He is a dog and he eats in his dog place. There's nothing nasty about it. This is just his place and he needs to know it.

You also have to consider your own human personality. Dominance problems tend to arise with the extremes of human personality – owners who are very aggressive themselves or those who are passive and nervous. You need to become very aware of your voice and body language. If you are always Mr or Ms Angry, with a shouty voice, getting in your dog's face and generally escalating a situation, your dog may feel the need to take you on in the end, as the fight element of its fight or flight behaviour during times of stress. So you need to gain self-control. Take the stress out of the situation. Make sure you and the dog have plenty of personal space. If it feels like you might both be kicking off, put your dog in his pen while you both calm down. Sometimes owners who are under a great deal of pressure themselves, or may even be going through a mental health problem, may have to take a step back from dog ownership for a while.

At the opposite end, very timid and passive owners do tend to get bossed by their dogs. In almost all cases this is not a problem because the dog doesn't have any interest in taking advantage of the situation. It's getting everything it wants, so why push it? But just occasionally an ambitious dog may decide to take it to the limit. Or there may be some subtle changes elsewhere in the household or in the dog's wider life that lead it down the aggression route. Dogs that do become aggressive are often responding to some general source of free-floating aggression within the household – if there are lots of arguments or crying. For the passive owner, it can be very difficult to learn to use your voice in a powerful assertive way, as with your body language. You just have to fake it till you make it! Find a private place and practise. Stamp your foot. Do a double teapot with hands on hips. Shout out loud. Growl! It may feel silly at first, but ultimately it is rather a liberating experience. As long as the dog's aggression is reasonably under control, the timid owner will also benefit tremendously from taking it along to obedience classes. There you can make new friends and discover that everybody has a dog problem at some time or another. There will almost certainly come a day when you think your dog biting you was the best thing that could have happened!

As we discussed in the opening section of this book, if the dog is actually seriously attacking, the time for retraining is passed. Protect yourself and any other humans or animals; handle the dog with great care to get it somewhere it can be more easily controlled (usually a travel crate or similar). Then at the first opportunity, take the dog to the vet to discuss the problem. I have never personally encountered such a situation and, take heart, it is extremely unlikely that you ever will.

No More Problems Any More

Part 3

The Canine Contract

From my experiences with many animals over the years – ranging all the way from the charismatic and gender-bending Harry the Hamster, through Bodge the brainiac horse, to Fergus the rescue cat, and of course all the different dogs – I have come to realise that when humans domesticate an animal we recruit it into our lives in one way or another, and likewise, we become some part of the animal's life, even if it is only feeding the birds. In doing this, a contract is created between us, not unlike the contract between employer and employee, or indeed in any relationship.

Whether the contract is legally binding or not, it exists, and both parties to the contract agree to accept each other's rights, as well as have their own expectations acknowledged. Whenever I see something going wrong with a domestic animal, and in the wild as well, the problem is usually due to some breakdown in this mutual contract between man and animal.

In India and parts of sub-Saharan Africa, there is a great issue in conserving populations of big cats, including leopards. Few people want to see a leopard shot, yet local humans, barely able to subsist, find leopards killing their goats and wish to destroy the leopards. But the increase in human population density in the area is what has forced the leopards to turn to goats as a prey. The contract between humans and leopards has been breached on both sides.

Both sides enjoying the Canine Contract.

Were this breach of contract ever to come before a court, the legal arguments would be well contestable by both sets of lawyers.

When it comes to us and our dogs: by buying, rescuing or adopting a dog in the first place, we have put in place a contract with the dog. As human beings, with all the assets of higher reasoning and functioning at our disposal, it is our responsibility to make sure the contract works for both sides. In my experience, dogs also seem to feel in some non-verbal way that they have a contract or bond with us, and most dogs take it very seriously. I find that if you are clear about your role and responsibilities in the contract, and fulfil them honestly, so will the dog. If you are uncommitted to the contract or treat it with contempt, this is where problems arise, just as they would with a contract between two humans.

Everybody's contract with their dog is different, but I've noted down the elements of the contract that my dogs regularly supply to me, and also the clauses that I consider my responsibility.

My Dog's Side of the Contract

Companionship is the primary reason dog owners all over the world mention for having their dog, and my dogs certainly fulfil this aspect of the contract. I cannot think of a single time (apart from ill-health) that my dogs haven't welcomed me with warmth.

Leisure enjoyment is a massive part of my life with my dogs. I love to walk and train them, and through competition I have met many wonderful people. I can well understand why research projects worldwide have shown that dog owners are less likely to suffer health problems.

Love is an anthropomorphic way of expressing the fact that dogs need to bond. Dogs have no word for this relationship, but humans tend to call it love or loyalty, and it is tremendously reassuring as a human to be on the receiving end of it, even if only from your four-legged friend!

Protection was one of the earliest clauses in the canine contract – guarding flocks and dwellings was almost certainly the primary reason mankind domesticated the dog in the first place, and many dogs still do this for a living. However, due to excess goofiness, I'm not sure whether I would rely on my dogs to protect me from much, although even they have been known to bark if a stranger is wandering around.

Commitment from a dog's point of view manifests itself as co-operation with human wishes, and contributes to their versatility and trainability.

Relaxation is mentioned by everybody I ask about why they love their dogs. Somehow, no matter how rubbish things are, taking your dog for a long walk always helps, and helps more than going for a walk on your own. Science supports this, to the extent that canine therapy is often used in hospitals and other care-giving centres.

Working Assistance may not be specifically relevant to you and your dogs, but all over the world dogs are working harder than ever to help humans, as assistance dogs; sniffers; search-and-rescuers; mine clearance; medical detection dogs; farm dogs; and country sports workers.

My Side of the Contract

Companionship is provided to me by the dogs, and I hope they get the same back from me. Particularly a lone dog, deprived by you, the human, of the comfort of a canine pack, needs the reassuring contact of a fellow 'pack member'. The dog relies on you to provide this. Don't just offer him companionship when you need it and then leave him high and dry while you are busy. Leaving a dog all alone for long hours is emotionally painful for a pack animal. If you are not going to be around much, make provision for your dog to get companionship from dog-walkers, sitters or neighbours, although, if possible, another dog is the best solution.

Freedom is my equivalent to the leisure enjoyment clause in the dogs' side of the contract. Through having dogs I get the freedom to access a huge range of new opportunities, but are the dogs getting something in return? Is their freedom equally enhanced by knowing me? We tend to assume that if we are going about our own lives freely, so is the dog. But from the dog's point of view this may not always be the case. For example, a dog that spends its entire life on a lead because it has not been taught basic obedience, is not as free as a dog that can be allowed to roam because its owner is confident it will return when asked. Try to think clearly about the life and routine your dog will have with you over the years, and work out how free that life will really be from the dog's point of view.

Health, care and well-being are absolutely fundamental to the contract. You decided to have a dog. Your dog is doing its bit. Now you need to keep your side of the bargain. With your own dog, you don't need me to remind you to house, feed, water, worm, groom, exercise and interact with him. I also like to try and do my bit for other dogs worldwide, who aren't lucky enough to have me as their servant, by researching and donating to canine charities. For more details on how to do this, check out the contacts section.

Protection is these days a more important responsibility for you towards your dogs than the other way round. Once dogs guarded us, but now our family dogs need us to protect them. Bear in mind the dangers of theft, traffic, other dogs and the environment.

Commitment is shown to you by your dog, and you have to match it on your side. In fact, I find that the need to show this commitment has actually become a tremendous positive in my life, as it creates a framework and sense of structure that helps me negotiate a sometimes hectic and stressful career as a busy writer and journalist. I think for many different reasons, individuals and families often find it helpful to have a positive, regular framework underlying daily life.

Respect is one of the mutual clauses of the contract that I most often find to be breached. Lack of respect is so often at the heart of dog problems. It is easy to assume that a problem has arisen because the dog does not respect the owner. In fact, at least as many problems are caused by the owner not respecting the dog! Respect is a two-way street and often the best way to earn it is by showing it yourself. So respect what your dog is, and be responsive to what his needs genuinely are, as opposed to what you might think he wants, and you will find that respect returned to you.

Fulfilment is something I consider very important to a dog's general well-being. A huge number of problems I come across are basically down to the dog being unfulfilled. Chewing and barking and all sorts of repetitive behaviours disappear quickly when your dog is fulfilled. It is a difficult aspect of your dog's life to evaluate, and all dogs are different in what and how much stimulation and challenge they need to fulfil them. My own dogs have what is called 'high drive' and consider any day wasted that has not included saving the world, winning a competition or, at the very least, finding several retrieves. Other types of dog might be satisfied with less. Try to ask yourself: has my dog genuinely had the chance to achieve all he is capable of doing or is he just sitting around bored and chewing the carpet in frustration?

The Canine Contract

Here's what we can EXPECT from our dogs		This is what we should OFFER our dogs	
Companionship	Dogs are loyal and rarely moody	Companionship	Like humans, dogs are social, group-dwelling animals and they need some form of companionship
Leisure enjoyment	Owning a dog opens massive opportunities for exercise and social activities	Freedom	How free is your dog really? Compared with you?
Love	The instinct to bond is very strong, and to us this comes across as love	Health and well-being	By keeping a dog as a pet you have made yourself responsible for this and shouldn't let him down
Protection	Both formally and informally, dogs offer this in many areas of our lives	Protection	Make sure your dog is safe from theft, accident, parasites and disease
Commitment	Most dogs are co-operative and highly committed to take part in all aspects of our lives	Commitment	We need to remember our responsibilities as dog owners
Relaxation	Playing and cuddling with your dog is a huge stress buster	Respect	As well as being your friend, your dog is an individual with his own needs and rights
Working Assistance	Millions of people world-wide rely on and benefit from the help of dogs working in everything from assistance to bomb disposal	Fulfilment	A dog is a living, thinking being and deserves to have a life at least as full as yours

Case History: Marco's Adopted Cocker

Marco needed a companion for his springer spaniel and ended up adopting the charming chocolate cocker spaniel, Jake. But then sadly, Marco's first dog died unexpectedly, which meant ... adopting another spaniel to keep Jake company! Rocci, the springer, and Jake now go everywhere with Marco. He says: 'Jake can be a bit of a handful, but it's worth it, the two dogs are lovely together, as their photo on a trip to the supermarket shows.'

Marco's spaniels, Rocci and Jake.

Time to go home for supper.

The SCIENCE BIT

A Glossary of Terms

Aggression Crisis – where a dog's aggressive behaviour poses an immediate threat to humans or other animals.

Anthropomorphism - interpreting animal behaviour from a human-centric point of view.

Attachment – the bond developed between a dog and its owner or immediate carer.

Attention-seeking – behaviour, good or bad, designed to illicit a response from the human.

Babesiosis– a dangerous disease caused by infection with Babesia Canis parasite carried by ticks.

Behaviour modification – the process of teaching/training where a dog's natural behaviours are adapted to suit human requirements (occasionally vice versa!).

Behaviour spectrum – the range of severity of symptoms/enactments of a particular behaviour issue.

Behavioural system – habitual responses developed in the dog as a result of experience or teaching, influenced by the brain's limbic system.

Compulsive behaviour – entrenched and often repeated activities over which the dog does not have conscious control, often developed in association with a particular behavioural system.

Coping mechanism – this is behaviour undertaken by the dog in order to help him cope with a situation he finds very stressful. Often these coping mechanisms are misunderstood as bad behaviour, e.g. growling.

Dehydration – dangerously low levels of fluid within the dog's tissues, usually due to lack of access to water, sometimes associated with renal failure and other health problems.

Displacement activity – a behaviour carried out by the dog semi-consciously in order to distract itself from a stressful situation.

Drive/high drive – A high motivation to perform challenging and stimulating activities, could be termed ambition.

Faulty reinforcement – the dog's owner unintentionally reinforces a dog's unwanted behaviour by giving it some form of satisfying feedback on its behaviour.

Fight or flight – a response to danger triggered within the primitive brain.

Food intolerance – impaired health (e.g. poor coat or digestion) due to eating foods unsuitable for dogs.

Hypo-allergenic – food ranges specifically designed not to trigger allergic or sensitive reactions in the dog's digestive system. Can also apply to products worn by the dog or applied to the skin.

Insecurity – a lack of a valid sense of safety or ability to trust care-givers.

Limbic system – the brain's 'operating system' mediating between the primitive brain and the neocortex. Considered to be the seat of motivation, emotion, learning and memory.

Lyme disease – a disease carried by ticks.

Maladaptation – confronted with difficult, stressful or unsafe situations, the dog develops a coping mechanism that has negative effects on itself and on the humans around it.

Motivation – the marked desire to perform in any number of ways including by learning, bonding and interacting with humans.

Neocortex – the most highly evolved part of the mammal brain, more highly developed in humans than other animals.

Neural Pathways – connect one part of the nervous system with another, specifically allowing learning and re-learning in the brain.

Pack Imperative – the need for a dog to relate well within a social structure.

Passive Aggression – a manipulative display of false fear in order to achieve a goal.

Primary Sense – the most important sense relied upon by an animal to experience its environment. In dogs this is the sense of smell.

Primitive/Reptilian Brain – the earliest part of the brain to develop, linked with basic survival functions.

217

Random Reward Theory/Random Incentivisation – a desired behaviour is rewarded only intermittently on a completely illogical basis, therefore creating a dependency in the subject. A form of brainwashing.

Reinforcement – a range of positive behaviours by the dog's owner/trainer designed to assist in forming new neural pathways in the dog's brain.

Repetitive behaviour – a form of compulsive or obsessive behaviour whereby the dog continuously repeats an activity (e.g. scratching) to the point where its normal life is compromised or health affected. Sometimes develops in inescapably stressful situations where an initial displacement activity does not achieve the necessary release and therefore becomes entrenched.

Sensory input – the full range of stimulations from the various senses.

Separation anxiety – a failure of bonding/attachment between the dog and owner usually caused by long absences of the owner. Often manifests in the dog not welcoming the owner on his return.

Stockholm syndrome – in human terms, this develops when captives are occasionally shown kindness by their captors and therefore develop dependency. In animals some trainers exploit this syndrome in order to achieve artificial training results.

Stress – evident in any animal which finds itself in a fearful situation it cannot control.

Trauma (chronic) – mental effects of prolonged exposure to trauma, which often continue after the traumatic situation has ceased.

Trauma (acute) – can relate to a physical injury or a transient fearful situation; does not persist.

Volition – Self-will, the ability to make choices based on the dog's own personal wants or needs.

Contacts for your Phone/Internet

RSPCA – To report cases of cruelty or distress phone **0300 1234 999**.

Your vet – Keep the surgery number, but more importantly, have the out-of-hours or locum number on speed dial.

The police – **999** for emergencies; **101** for assistance; importantly, know the number of your neighbourhood officer, as he will very often be clued in to all sorts of dog emergencies.

The council dog warden – Your local authority will have a dog warden, whose responsibility it is to collect information about missing dogs or other dog problems in the area. However, due to local government spending cuts in the UK, accessibility to dog wardens is very restricted in some areas. To find the details of your local dog warden, visit **www.animalwardens.co.uk**.

Dog search organisations – Some dog search organisations are charitable and free to use, though welcome a small donation. There are also local networks that use text and email trees to alert lost dogs. Various commercial dog detective agencies also exist, which will charge a fee, but can be useful as intermediaries in the recovery of stolen dogs. Start by looking at **www.animalsearchuk.co.uk** or **www.lostdogsuk.co.uk**. If you belong to a breed society or working club with your dog, their network can also be very helpful.

Canine Contacts

General: The Kennel Club, UK is at **www.thekennelclub.org.uk**, where you will find a huge amount of information, including many links to other useful websites. For the websites of breed clubs of your favourite types of dog, just click on 'breed information centre' at the Kennel Club website. **www.discoverdogs.org.uk** gives information about the Kennel Club's special dog show to introduce newcomers to the world of dogs. The American Kennel Club is at **www.akc.org**, and also very helpful for information and links across the USA, but bear in mind that different states often have different arrangements. Crufts Dog Show, the world's most famous, is at **www.crufts.org.uk**.
The Companion Dog Club created for non-pedigree dogs can be found at **www.thekennelclub.org.uk/activities/companion-dog-shows**. Organised for non-pedigrees at Crufts, is Scruffts dog show; check out **www.crufts.org.uk/scruffts**.

For non-pedigree dogs competing in various fields the Activity Register is kept by the Kennel Club, **www.thekennelclub.org.uk/registration**.

Health: For information about vets in the UK, go to the profession's website at **www.bva.co.uk**. Various dog welfare charities may be able to help with vets' fees, etc, and if you are worried about a health issue you can get in touch. Visit these websites: **www.pdsa.org.uk**; **www.dogstrust.org.uk**; **www.bluecross.org.uk**; **www.pets4homes.co.uk**; **www.rspca.org.uk**.

Equipment: All sorts of dog accessories, including beds, indoor kennels, etc, try **www.canineconcepts.co.uk** or **www.petplanet.co.uk** and in the USA **www.wayfair.com** (which also ships internationally). Good quality car travelling pens can be found at **www.lintran.co.uk** or **www.canineconcepts.co.uk**. One of the leading indoor dog loo brands is the Ugodog indoor dog litter tray; you can also try **www.piddleplace.com** in the USA. Among the best places to get training accessories online are **www.sportingsaint.co.uk** (ships worldwide) and **www.traininglines.co.uk**. Additional training accessories are available from **www.questgundogs.co.uk** who supply Air Kong training dummies, and see the full Kong range at the website: **www.kongcompany.com**.

Dog Charities: The UK's leading dog charities are **www.dogstrust.org.uk**; **www.four-paws.org.uk**; **www.homes4dogs.co.uk** and **www.dogpages.org.uk**. Also check out **www.battersea.org.uk** for details of events in aid of the Battersea Dogs Home. In America, one of the main sites is **www.animalcharitiesofamerica.org**.

Dog Walkers: The dog walkers' professional body in the UK is the Association of Professional Dog Walkers, **www.apdw.co.uk**; and in America it is the American National Association of Professional Pet Sitters **www.petsitters.org**.